HOME

AT THE OFFICE

HOME
AT THE OFFICE

WORKING REMOTELY AS A WAY OF LIFE

BARBORI GARNET

atmosphere press

To my mother, Barboria. Thank you for your unending love, support, encouragement, and wisdom.

Disclaimer

Although the publisher and the author have made every effort to ensure that the information in this book was correct at press time and while this publication is designed to provide accurate information in regard to the subject matter covered, the publisher and the author assume no responsibility for errors, inaccuracies, omissions, or any other inconsistencies herein and hereby disclaim any liability to any party for any loss, damage, or disruption caused by errors or omissions, whether such errors or omissions result from negligence, accident, or any other cause.

This publication is meant as a source of valuable information for the reader, however it is not meant as a substitute for direct expert assistance. If such level of assistance is required, the services of a competent professional should be sought.

Table of Contents

Part 3: Hands-on Workbook: Is Remote Work Right for You?

Appendix A – Articles

Appendix B - Resources

A Little Help from Friends and Readers
Index
Acknowledgements

Foreword by Cyndi Ball

In 2009, I officially began my home-based, entrepreneurial journey on my 7-acre homestead in the southeast United States. Each step to build my business was in answer to a need that had arisen. Each answer produced more questions and pretty soon I was running a successful, farm-based business! I was providing income for my family from my passion for homesteading. Maybe I shouldn't admit this but I didn't have a plan when I started – one idea led to another, lots of tweaking, failed attempts, multiple iterations of a single idea and soon I was running a multi-faceted, diverse homestead business! And I loved my "job"! As Barbori states in her book, start with a passion. If you do what you love, you will never work a day in your life.

In 2020, my life took a major turn and I had to sell the farm and with the farm went my business. I found myself applying for a "job." Granted, my acceptance of the offer brought me to beautiful Montana, but I hadn't worked outside of the home for 30 years! My last corporate position had been in 1987. And here I was conforming my life to 8 hours a day, the hours dictated by the owner of the business. I felt trapped in the confines of corporate thinking and management. Admittedly, it has been a rude awakening in comparison to running my own business, working hours most conducive to my productivity, and being outside most of my "work" day. But you know what? My entrepreneurial spirit arises and I am more motivated than ever to create a new business to afford me the opportunity to work from home again – home being a trailer so I can travel! I do have a plan this time and I'm putting in the hours to make this dream come true.

Reading Barbori's book, *Home at the Office: Working Remotely as a Way of Life*, has added fuel to my entrepreneurial fervor to create a business again that gives me the freedom I once knew. Her work is one of the most thorough, comprehensive books on this subject I have read. The details she covers are unbelievable! Barbori's ideas and suggestions are noteworthy.

The interviews with other owners of home-based businesses are inspirational. I wish this book had been around in 2009 when I started my own farm-based business. The information would have saved me a lot of misguided effort and mistakes.

If you're looking for a road map to get you to your destination of a home-based business, pick up this book and read it, take notes, and implement the truths of success needed to make a dream come true.

- Cyndi Ball, Founder and Executive Director of
National Ladies Homestead Gathering,
and author of *Simplify Your Homestead Plan:
A Workbook* for *Setting Goals That Make Sense*

Preface

Freedom. Flexibility. Independence. That is what I love about working from home. You can choose whether you start your own business, work for a company, or do a combination of both. You can work from home at any age and stage of life: as a recent university or college graduate who wants to travel the world; as a parent who wants to take their children to and from school while still making an income and maintaining professional ties; or as a retiree who wants to work a few months of the year and have time to visit family and friends or spend time on hobbies. That is what I want for you. I want you to have those same choices and options. And working from home gives you exactly that.

How did I come to work from home? It began with being homeschooled and continuing through to and beyond high school. As I grew, I learned more and tried new things. Freedom, flexibility, and independence became important elements of my life. Whether in my career choice, hobbies, or interests, I was looking for those features.

After five years of trying public, separate, and private schools without much success due to bullying, peer pressure, and teacher issues (some of which included grading on a bell curve as early as grade two and not providing all homework or information) encountered in the various schools, I was homeschooled from grade five to the end of high school. During each year of being homeschooled, I became more independent and planned out how many lessons I needed to do each week to finish the textbook by the end of the school year. I also learned to be a creative and independent thinker and take the self-initiative to start work and complete it on time. All this helped, and continues to help me tremendously, in solving problems and having the get-up-and-go to take the first step to get things done.

This independence stayed with me. At the age of 18, having experienced one year of working outside the home at a job in the food industry, I decided to begin teaching violin and piano lessons. While I enjoyed meeting new people and making friends with some of my co-workers, I realized that I preferred to be able to set my own schedule — I wanted that freedom and flexibility. I also recognized that I had the knowledge, skills, and love of playing music to share with and pass on to others.

Since then, I have added more offerings to my business including playing violin at weddings and special events and selling items on my websites' e-store. Being a business owner and working from home is not easy. There are many challenges to overcome but even more vital than overcoming challenges in determining success in business is having or developing the ability to adapt. This means being open to adding or changing things as needed, learning new skills, thinking creatively, and not giving up when the going gets tough.

In addition to owning my own business and working from home, I have worked for periods of time as an employee and on contracts for companies. I view those work times and contracts as avenues through which to meet new people, gain new knowledge, and supplement my income.

Below is a list of the many different types of work I have done from home, both in my own businesses and working for companies, or on contract:
- Writer
- Sales Rep
- Artist
- Pet Sitting
- Music Instructor
- Marketing Assistant
- Social Media and Research Work
- Website Creation and Admin Work

My reasons for working from home since 2010 and continuing to make that choice going forward include having a flexible schedule, using my creativity to find innovative solutions for my business and work, and spending my time on work and interests that I enjoy.

The freedom of a flexible schedule means I can go on a daytrip during the week to avoid the weekend crowds, feel professionally fulfilled, avoid the hassle and stress of a commute by transit or being stuck in a car during rush hour, and spend time with family and friends when it fits into my schedule.

Thinking of and implementing creative solutions for my business and work allows me to grow and develop my companies in a way that works for my career goals. I can focus my energy toward building the vision I have for my work in the coming years and decades.

Being able to live a life that I enjoy in the present means that I am excited to wake up every day, ready for what lies ahead. I am not counting down the days and years to retirement; instead, I am living each day to the fullest because I enjoy what I do and I get to do what I find fulfilling. Although there are challenges, deadlines, and many tasks to accomplish, the feeling of control and the ability to make needed changes allows me to reduce stress to a manageable level and avoid chronic stress.

Reminding myself of all those reasons helps me to persevere through the difficult times and setbacks that life will inevitably bring. It keeps me thankful and happy that I get to work from home — not because I have to but because I want to.

All this, and more, is what I want for you.

Introduction

Home at the Office: Working Remotely as a Way of Life has been designed to give you, the reader, an outline to create your home office and identify the remote work that is best suited to your needs, home environment, work goals, and life.

The book is organized into three sections to make the information presented easy and enjoyable to read, find sections of the most interest, and practically apply the advice.

The first section, *Part 1: Making Working from Home Work for You,* begins with showing that working from home is a way of life. It should blend with all areas of your life and should be an activity that you look forward to, rather than dread. Yes, remote work does require discipline, long hours, and hard work. However, you can set your hours, diversify your income, and work from wherever you have an internet connection.

The rest of *Part 1* covers areas of interest and importance to successfully work remotely. Examples include the elements of a home office and how to have fun personalizing your office space, working from home during different ages and stages of life, and assessing your technology to meet work requirements.

In the second section, *Part 2: Extraordinary People Who Work from Home,* you will be introduced to people across North America who successfully work from home. You will read their stories and gain insight from their words of wisdom. By reading what they share, the goal is for you to be encouraged and inspired in pursuing your own remote work, knowing that you can make it through any and every challenge or obstacle which comes your way.

The third section, *Part 3: Hands-on Workbook - Is Remote Work Right for You?* gives a hands-on area to explore your thoughts and ideas. Questions are posed for you to consider and think about with space provided to record your answers.

It may be helpful to view this section as an opportunity to learn about different aspects related to working from home which you may not have previously considered. You are also encouraged to use this part of the book to write down thoughts which may come as you read through.

Whether you start reading the book from page one or somewhere further along in the book, my hope is that you will feel confident that you, too, can work remotely in a way which blends in with all areas of your life. May you find freedom, flexibility, and independence when you choose to work from home.

Part One

Make Working from Home Work for You

Working from Home as a Way of Life

The value of work and what it provides or affords means a variety of things to people. For some, working means providing the necessities like food, shelter, and clothing. For others, it means being able to afford to travel and go on vacation. Working can also mean saving for retirement, buying a home, saving for a child's education, and more. And for others, work gives their life a purpose and significance, and gives them tasks and a routine to look forward to each day.

Because work affects our lives in many ways, it is important that it enables us to live the way that we envision and that is right for us. Work should not be a pursuit that leaves us feeling drained or makes us stressed just thinking about going to work the next day. In fact, it should be quite the opposite. Work must be an occupation that raises us up and brings us energy when we engage in its activities, whether that is for a few short hours or several hours long. It should be an engaging activity which blends in, rather than clashes, with other aspects of our lives.

That is what working from home is — it is work that fits with how and where you live, and with whom you live. Working from home allows you to design and complement your work environment with the rest of your personal reality: family, friends, hobbies, goals, and all.

It is a Way of Life
A Way of Life

Working from home is a way of life. It gives you, the individual, as much freedom of choice, flexibility, and independence as possible. You can choose how many hours a week to work, whether 10, 20, or 35 hours. It gives

> "Working from home is a way of life. It gives you, the individual, as much freedom of choice, flexibility, and independence as possible."

you flexibility to decide when you want to work — the time of day, the days, or parts of the year.

Independence is yours by giving you the choice to work from home as a business owner, as a freelancer, on contract, or for a company. In self-employed remote work as a way of life, you will also need to exercise independence in making decisions on what business services and products to offer and being open to adapting as circumstances change.

If you have previously worked at jobs where nine to five was expected, it may be overwhelming to think about the choice you have in deciding how many hours and what time of the day you want to work. For now, begin to notice what times of the day you are most focused, most productive, and do your best work, or when you are drained of energy. Later in this book, we will talk more about finding your natural biorhythm and making it flow into your life.

Time

We are each gifted with the same 24 hours in a day to get things done and engage in personally fulfilling activities. How we use the time we are given is what matters and what will ultimately make a difference.

The beautiful thing about working from home is that it gives you more hours to allocate as you see fit. There will be time saved commuting and fewer long or unnecessary meetings.

How are you going to use the extra time you now have control over, even if it is just 30 minutes or one hour each day? Would you enjoy unrushed mealtimes with your family, drop off and pick up the kids from school, develop a hobby or further grow your business, or go outside for a walk, hike, a game of tennis, or garden?

Perhaps, by working from home, you may decide to work part-time outside the home. This may provide you with the perfect balance of interacting with others while also being there for family. Or maybe, by getting to know your kids as you work from home, you might decide that homeschooling would be a good idea for them and the whole family. Whatever it is that you want to do, remote work will give you the time needed to do it.

By working from home and having more hours in the day to do things that are important to you, your life will become richer, more meaningful, and less stressful. Gone will be waiting for the weekends to come around and instead, you will be looking forward to working and enjoying life each day. All you need to decide is how you are going to use the time that has been given to you.

Mindset

Working from home is a mindset. It means that you realize that you have options. You are never stuck. Even though it may not seem or feel like it, you are always moving forward. There may be setbacks or discouragement along the way but you learn from these and keep going. You know what you want and you do your best not to let anything stop you in the process of achieving it.

Being creative and using your ingenuity, knowledge, and experience to look for opportunities, find solutions, and moving past obstacles, challenges, and defeats are all part of having the right frame of mind. Having a positive and open mindset

> "Being creative and using your ingenuity, knowledge, and experience to look for opportunities, find solutions, and moving past obstacles, challenges, and defeats are all part of having the right frame of mind."

where you recognize that you have opportunities waiting for you just around the corner can make working from home — and your life — that much more of a success. Some tools to use in supporting a positive mindset include exercise, journaling, a vision board, prayer, and meditation.

Resilient and Ready for Challenges

As challenging times in the world show us, most recently seen during the Coronavirus pandemic in 2020, being able to adapt in work and life is essential not just to survive but even to thrive. In difficult circumstances, access to regular work and income, nourishing food and clean drinking water, and safe housing are keys to resiliency.

In the United States, "Even before the coronavirus outbreak forced businesses across the world to adopt a remote work policy, there were over 5 million U.S. employees working from home at least half the time. Now, telecommuting is more popular than ever—whether people were prepared for it or not."[1]

According to Statistics Canada, "Nearly five million Canadians started working from home in response to measures to prevent the spread of COVID-19, and a new poll finds that many workers think the change will be permanent. Statistics

Canada found that 4.7 million Canadians who don't normally work from home started to in response to the pandemic, based on a survey conducted the week of March 22 [2020]. When the agency added in all of the workers who normally work from home, the athleisure-clad masses pecking at laptops in living rooms and participating in video meetings swelled to 6.8 million people, or nearly 40 per cent of Canada's workforce."[2]

Perhaps one of the most important things is that working from home allows you to keep on working. As long as you have access to a secure and reliable internet connection, you are prepared to work from just about anywhere. This can make a world of difference as it could mean that you will have more options for a reliable source of income coming in during changing times, whether you work for a company or have your own business.

And while you work remotely, why not show your support for others who work from home? Start by buying locally in your city, then within your province/state, and next nationally within your country. Whether it is food, clothes and shoes, stationery, kitchen and household products, electronics, or something else, you will not only be acquiring quality products which are more locally sourced, made, and sold but also helping to strengthen and diversify the economy.

Have Confidence and Visualize Yourself Being Successful

This is paramount to you achieving the success and goals that you want to reach by working from home. To begin, picture yourself as someone who is confident no matter what and who has lots to offer. Approaching your journey to remote work with all the confidence that you can summon will reflect positively on your path to success. Using affirmations in the morning, at noon, and at night, tell yourself that you are confident in yourself and have lots to offer.

Next, visualize yourself as already employed in the type of

remote work that you want to do, whether as a small business owner, freelancer, or working for a company. Seeing yourself in this way confirms it not only in your conscious but also in your subconscious mind. As a result, you will be guided and led to the decisions and actions you need to take to achieve the image that you have set for yourself. Repeat this successful image of yourself — being already employed in remote work — several times a day.

Every morning, afternoon, and evening, straighten your shoulders and lift your head high with confidence and believe in yourself. Visualize yourself successfully employed working from home, and you will attain the image you have set for yourself. Write down your goal, in one sentence, on a piece of paper so that you can read and see it each and every day. And remember to be as specific as possible with what you visualize and by what date you want to achieve things.

Addressing Fears

If remote work is something new to you, there may be hesitations or fears encountered in the beginning. Do a little research and take the time to read about some of the issues which you may face so that you feel prepared in these areas for what may come: source of potential clients, socialization, support of family and friends, working from home because you have to, technology concerns, and having the skills it takes to work remotely. If there are other concerns that you have, in addition to these, knowing what those are is part of being prepared. Resolve them as much as possible, and then advance with confidence one step at a time as you start working from home.

Source of Potential Clients

Giving thought to how you will find clients will assist you as you begin to work from home and in establishing an income stream. Trying different places and ways – social media, e-mail marketing, word-of-mouth – to reach clients will provide insight as to which method produces the most response and leads to paid work. As you continue working remotely, you will fine tune your marketing plan and learn where your source of potential clients is greatest. For now, having some kind of plan in place will help to alleviate this fear.

Socialization

Many people are social, to a greater or lesser degree, and desire or seek out social interactions. This is a normal part of the day-to-day world as people spend much of the time talking, asking questions, and learning from others. By removing themselves from the physical workplace, some people may fear that they will lose or miss out on the social interactions found in an office setting. To a certain extent, it is true that working from home will probably change the social dynamics and interactions as most work is done through technology. But do not let this discourage you.

Instead, look for ways to connect and interact with others even when you work from home. For example, each Monday morning you could phone someone else. Decide ahead of the call how long the conversation will take so as not to encroach on your work time and ask them how their weekend went and what their goals are for the workweek ahead. It will certainly get the day and week off to a great start and you will get to know others better. It may also provide you with needed encouragement and accountability in accomplishing work tasks. Or maybe you can join or help organize a virtual event where you, and other people who

> "Finding unique and meaningful ways to socially engage and interact will be a huge help in making working from home enjoyable."

work from home, can socialize with each other through a fun activity. Finding unique and meaningful ways to socially engage and interact will be a huge help in making working from home enjoyable.

Support of Family and Friends

The support of family and friends can play an important role in work success. Take the steps needed to get family members to pitch in and friends to cheer you on. Perhaps creating a weekly menu where everyone can see what is for dinner, and who is making which meal, will minimize interruptions and let you finish work. Maybe ordering groceries online and having them delivered to your home means less time spent on errands, more time spent with loved ones and friends, and more support for your working. If cleaning the house is slowing you down, hire someone to clean your home on a regular basis or ask your family to pitch in. Even though it may be easier said than done, take the action necessary to make your home life and social life run smoothly.

When it comes to working, you do not want to be distracted by all the things which need to be done at home. You want your focus to be on making sure that working from home is working for you.

Working from Home Because You Have To

What do you do if you have to work from home because you have to, either temporarily or permanently, rather than because you want to or choose to? What if, by working from home, you find that you are spending too much time at home, to the point of feeling cooped up? Here are a few things to consider:

- Consider getting outside of your home office throughout the day—can you go for a walk or jog or meet with a friend over lunch hour or just sit on your balcony or in

the backyard soaking in the sunshine?
- Would having a regular morning routine and a regular daily schedule throughout the day help with knowing what to expect? Most days, my morning routine consists of:
  - A walk
  - A little bit of reading
  - Around 10 minutes of rebounding
  - A glass or two of lemon water
  - Later during the day, I play a few pieces on the piano, write, and do stretches, strength exercises, and weights. By starting my day with a routine, not only do I know what to expect but I also begin by focusing on me and giving myself the gift of health and exercise.
- If working from home is really not working for you, even after trying the above suggestions, then see if you can work in an office setting for part of the time like every other day or two days a week.

Technology Concerns

Concerns about technology might influence your consideration and confidence in doing remote work. You may wonder whether you have the right equipment to start working remotely or if you need to upgrade. To address this fear, it is best to check if you have the following:
- A computer which has good speed in booting up, connecting to the internet, and downloading documents
- A solid security system to keep your computer safe from viruses and virus attacks
- Reliable internet connection

Reviewing the above basics will be a good place to start in having the technology needed to work from home. After that, it will depend on the kind of work you do and whether you need a printer/scanner/fax, camera, iPad, or other specific software or technological equipment.

To Have What It Takes

Over the course of your education and work experience, you have learned and acquired many valuable and important skills and developed personal character traits to help ensure your success at work and in life. Looking at the list below, notice which of these traits you already possess and which ones you need to spend more time improving. These skills and qualities can help determine whether you already have what it takes to work from home or whether you need to focus on developing your skills in certain areas before or while taking that leap:

> "Over the course of your education and work experience, you have learned and acquired many valuable and important skills and developed personal character traits to help ensure your success at work and in life."

- Self-starter
- Passion
- Optimism
- Perseverance
- Creativity
- Leadership
- Planning skills
- Dedication
- Organization
- Self-discipline
- Determination
- Ability to work independently
- Confidence
- Ability to adapt

- Willingness to learn new things
- Time management skills

To begin, start by asking yourself and assessing when in the past you found yourself in situations or moments, however brief and inconsequential, when you showed these inclinations.

For example, creativity—was there a time when you offered to help create clever storage solutions for a small space or you saw a problem and already knew how to solve it? Or if you really wanted to do something, were there examples where you rearranged your schedule to be able to participate? You do not need to be creative in the way an artist is creative, but you need to have enough of that gift to find solutions to problems.

Other questions to ask yourself during this self-assessment include:

1) Do you have the self-discipline to get work done without someone looking over your shoulder or checking to make sure that you have completed your work on time?

2) Do you have the persistence to create and develop multiple streams of income, even when facing disappointment or feeling discouraged?

3) Do you have the perseverance to keep on searching, looking for, and creating the type of work that fits your interest, skills, preferred hours, or lifestyle?

4) Do you have the time management skills to keep tasks on track and finish projects early and on time?

5) Do you have the support and encouragement of at least some family members and friends?

6) Do you have the creativity to come up with solutions when you find problems, see where changes need to be made, and the confidence to implement those solutions once you come up with them?

All the above require a self-confidence that you can do the

work, a need to acquire knowledge and experience as you go, and a willingness to adapt and change.

If you hesitated in answering yes to any of the questions or are in doubt as to your strength in some areas, take the time to develop and improve in those areas now. What are a few ways to gain the above skills and qualities? Try these to begin with:

1) Do you see something in your current work, or at home, that needs to be improved? Instead of waiting to be told, be a self-starter and approach the appropriate person (a client or colleague if it is work-related or a partner if it is home-related) about the improvement you want to implement, get their approval, and then get on the job to get it done. If you do not get their okay, you can still take the initiative to negotiate, to highlight benefits, and open the door to make the change happen.

2) Do you need more self-discipline? Take a few online classes that have assignments to submit by certain deadlines. This will help develop self-motivation to start work on time, work on tasks little by little, and submit work in the assigned time frame. Developing self-discipline means that you can do the work on your own without having a boss or teacher constantly checking your work.

3) Another benefit of taking online classes is that it can significantly increase your time management skills. When all you have is an upcoming submission deadline, it will be up to you to determine when during the day and week you take an hour or two to work on the assignment to get it done. However, because people have lots on the go in their lives, finding and making time in their schedule is not always easy. One place to begin is by identifying your priorities or blocking in

time — that will go a long way to focusing in on what is important and help you manage your time better.

4) Does it seem that the idea for a remote work business is taking too long to appear? Or is it taking too much time to implement a remote work business idea that will be profitable? Do not give up. This will increase your <u>perseverance</u> and <u>planning skills</u>. Going through the steps and processes to come up with a business idea which people will need and which you enjoy working on takes time and patience. Keep at it by thinking what you like to do, what you are good at, do research, and look for a problem which potential customers need to have solved. Once you come up with a business concept, start working on setting up the business. Are you thinking that this sounds like it is as much work as finding the right person to be your life partner? You can be the judge of that.

In my pursuit of growing my skills, I developed excellent time management by taking classes online as part of my undergraduate and graduate degrees. Through my education and volunteering, I have been able to take on leadership roles. This meant that I had to be a self-starter in some cases and persevere in others. In business, I have tried new marketing ideas and offered new products, some of which worked and others which did not work so well. Rather than being discouraged at the first sign of difficulty, the important takeaway is that I have tried, adjusted and implemented a change, and learned along the way.

There are several avenues available and open to honing the skills and qualities you need to work on. The key is to be creative and find the opportunities that are not only at your current skill level but that also allow you to take your skills and abilities to the next stage. You might find that going to a job resource centre, career fair, or reading books and magazines to gain new knowledge and skills may be helpful. Whichever step you need to take to get to the next level in your skills and abilities, take the opportunity and pursue it.

Working from home is a wonderful way of life. When any fears or concerns are understood and addressed, be they socialization, support of family and friends, or having the needed qualities and skills, then there is room to truly embrace the independent and creative mindset, the gift of time, and the flexible lifestyle which comes by way of remote work.

Takeaway Tips

Working from home is...

- ✓ Enjoying a flexible way of life
- ✓ Having an independent and creative mindset
- ✓ Using time efficiently
- ✓ Being resilient, adaptable, and ready for change
- ✓ Having confidence and visualizing yourself being successful

Challenges to overcome may include...

- Socialization
- Support of family and friends
- Necessity rather than choice of working from home
- Technology concerns
- Development of the skills and qualities it takes to successfully work from home

Types of Working from Home and Legal Structure Options

In this chapter, seven different types of working from home will be presented. Each has its own advantages and drawbacks but you can combine them to achieve the best blend of features. Even though some are geared more toward working remotely for a company, it is important to be familiar with as many variations as possible. This ensures that you have the information you need to make informed decisions.

Take the time to read and think over what is covered here as you consider your next action steps in working from home.

There are at least seven types of working from home options:

1) The preparation and selling of food-based items or products made in-home but sold in stores
2) Services provided at home to customers who come to a home office or studio e.g., dayhome provider, accountant, music teacher, hairdresser, massage therapist, yoga studio teacher, etc.
3) Services, information, or products provided entirely online
4) Businesses which hire contractors on their behalf

(different from employees) to work on projects or other work as required

5) Businesses which hire employees who then, in turn, contact prospective clients with the goal of bringing business in

6) Employees who work from home for a business

7) Consultants who work on contract for universities, corporations, etc. from home

1) *The preparation and selling of food-based items or products made in-home but sold in stores:*

Food-based businesses are one avenue through which to work from home if you enjoy working with food. In the United States, each state has different regulations to look into and understand which can be found by searching 'Cottage Food Laws' or a similar heading. These laws and regulations govern food safety standards and the type of food made in a home kitchen.

Examples of business bylaws may include limiting food items made to jams, pies, and breads, the location where food products can be sold, and the amount of income you can make each year from a food-based business at home.

In Canada, the regulations may be more complex while at the same time being less defined for what is required in starting a food-based business at home. In recent years, it appears that changes have been made to regulate the size of production. For example, once production grows beyond the capacity of a home kitchen, there is a requirement to use a commercial kitchen space to produce the food items.

The many aspects to food-based businesses include following up on administration tasks such as responding to e-mails, phone calls, and website orders, posting photos, updates, events, and specials on social media, and updating website information; the making of the food items or products in a home kitchen or renting a commercial kitchen at the same time each week or month to make the food items; and delivering and distributing the food items directly to customers or taking the items to stores which will then sell them to their customers.

Depending on how much time and resources you have, you can grow your food-based home business through many means and avenues: taking custom orders, catering events (reunions, weddings, retreats, conferences, meetings, birthdays, bachelor/bachelorette and retirement parties, graduations, anniversaries, baby showers, etc.), leading workshops and classes on the preparation and selling of food and food items, consulting/teaching about proper food preparation and nutrition, and even possibly franchising or opening a factory for producing your food items.

2) *Services provided at home to customers who come to a home office or studio e.g., dayhome provider, accountant, music teacher, hairdresser, massage therapist, yoga studio teacher, etc.:*

Some work in a variety of fields and have the skills, knowledge, and expertise, and also prefer, to work from home while providing a wide range of much-needed services to customers who come to their home. In addition to the above service providers, others include makeup artist, realtor, fitness/yoga instructor, art teacher, and more.

"In services provided at home, it is important to consider which room or part of the house will be used for providing the service…and to think about how it will affect other family members and the flow of their routines, habits, and schedules."

In services provided at home, it is important to consider which room or part of the house will be used for providing the service so that it is easily accessible to clients (having bathroom facilities close by is a good idea) and that, preferably, clients do not have to go through or past private areas (like bedrooms) of the home.

Whether constructing or buying a home and providing a service from home starting tomorrow or in 10 years, the best solution is to make your decision on the design of the home with these things in mind so that the space to provide the service from home is ready and available when needed.

When considering which space in the home clients will come into as your home office or studio, make sure to think about how it will affect other family members and the flow of their routines, habits, and schedules. For example, will family members need to leave the area and go to the basement or a bedroom while you meet with clients? If yes, are you meeting with clients during dinnertime when your family would prefer to be able to make meals and eat in the kitchen and dining room area but instead have to disrupt their dinnertime by either eating elsewhere in the house or eating early such as at 4 p.m. or eating late such as at 8 p.m.?

Analyzing the daily routines of yourself and your family will help determine the best space in your home to use as an office or studio while minimizing any disruption and maximizing everyone's happiness.

For services provided at home, it is a good idea to have at least one, and maybe even two, parking spots either on your driveway or in front of your house available for your clients to use. It will be convenient for them and will keep you in good stead with your neighbors. If you live in a climate which receives snow during the winter, make sure that you keep your driveway and any pathways clear of snow for when clients come. If the snow melts and then freezes, turning to ice, throw sand onto the ice patches so that no clients slip, fall, or hurt themselves.

When you are deciding on providing a service at home, do your research into what is required. Do you need to incorporate or is being a sole proprietor fine for your needs and purposes? Do you need to get a business license or not? What kind of insurance do you need?

Having these answers ahead of time will help you determine if providing a service at home is the best choice for your circumstances as well as give you an idea of additional expenses (incorporation fees, business insurance, renovation costs, air cleaner, etc.) related to a home business.

3) *Services, information, or products provided entirely online:*

Services, information, or products which are provided entirely online can also be run as a home-based business. The difference here is that all work is done through the computer (using the internet) and phone. Perhaps your customers download items directly from your website and most payments are made through Stripe, PayPal, e-transfer, or some other e-commerce setup.

Having an online remote job means that there are no or rarely any customers, clients, or students coming to a home office. You might need to meet with your clients in-person every so often and have the occasional face-to-face meeting with a client at their place of work or over lunch but otherwise, work can be completed primarily online and over the phone.

4) *Businesses which hire contractors on their behalf (different from employees) to work on projects or other work as required:*

Another type of work-from-home business is a business which hires contractors on its behalf to get work done. Hiring contractors can be for a period of employment that lasts from six to twelve months (or shorter or longer as needed). Some of the reasons a business may hire contractors to work include: covering a maternity or parental leave; needing a specific area of research or expertise; a temporary high business volume during a busy time; giving students the opportunity to gain experience through a summer job as part of a government grant or program; and covering an interim position while the company advertises and looks for a permanent employee to take over the position on a part-time or full-time basis.

While simultaneously allowing the business owner and other employees to work from home, or maybe the business has a physical office location while allowing contractors to work remotely, contractors might be called on to help for a specific project because of experience and expertise needed for the success and completion of a project. Examples of work contractors could be engaged for include social media, website, engineering, bookkeeping, analysis, and more.

While contractors working from home for the business may not be directly contacting customers for new business, the work that the contractors do may have various goals such as:

- Bringing in new business to the company through increasing web presence and other advertising avenues
- Increasing visibility through media coverage by completing the project
- Increasing the likelihood of getting new work by submitting a successful project bid or helping to make the company run smoother and more efficiently with the result being higher profits, expansion, and more new business
- Or any combination of the above three
5) *Businesses which hire employees who then, in turn, contact prospective clients with the goal of bringing business in:*

Some businesses hire employees whose job it is to contact prospective clients. Examples of these are positions such as Sales Consultants, Sales Advisors, Account Managers, Business Development Managers, Product Advisors, Product Managers, and others. These roles can be responsible for tasks as varied as finding students to fill courses in professional development, continuing education, and post-secondary courses to selling ad space in magazines, newspapers, and newsletters. Employees may be provided with a list or a database of prospective clients to call on and close sales or find new prospects leading to sales. Remuneration might be a straight commission or a combination of base salary plus commission on each sale gained and closed or a bonus might be offered if a certain number of sales are reached in a week, month, or quarter.

Employees who contact prospective clients can make calls and send e-mails from home while based anywhere around the world. In my experience, it can be made to work where the company office is based in one city while its employees work from home in the same city or in other cities across the country and in different time zones (e.g., Mountain Standard, Eastern Standard, and Atlantic Standard Time). The key to ensure smooth coordination between employees and owners or managers could be a combination of regular communication, weekly employee teleconference meetings to stay up to date on employee and company sales goals and for additional sales training, and keeping in mind the difference in time zones when reaching out to colleagues.

If employees are working from home making calls, they will most likely be working from a database, such as Salesforce or another program, with access to it provided by the business. The Salesforce program is just one of several which can be used for logging calls made, scheduling follow-up calls that need to be made, and keeping track of any notes or follow-up actions that need to be taken such as sending a prospect an e-mail with more information on the product, service, or course being offered.

6) Employees who work from home for a business:

Then there are employees working from home for a business. This is different from the one presented above in that the employee is not reaching out to and calling potential and current clients to bring in business but is doing necessary "background" or administrative work which can include the likes of preparing plans and bids for projects, maintaining an up-to-date web presence, and ensuring notes and files are recorded and entered properly.

Employees working from home for a business can complete their work without needing to contact clients as a regular part of their day-to-day job. The type of work they might be doing includes computer programming, drafting and design work, marketing, copywriting and editing, secretarial work, accounting, and more. Put another way, employees working from home for a business work more on the behind-the-scenes tasks or those things that clients have ordered rather than be responsible for actively prospecting and bringing in new business.

Staying well-organized and on top of tasks, plus regular communication with co-workers and managers, are the secrets to success in being an employee who works from home for a business.

7) Consultants who work on contract for universities, corporations, etc. from home:

Finally, the seventh and last type of working from home is the group of consultants who work on a contract basis for various employers such as universities, corporations, companies, government organizations, company boards, and more.

In uncertain economies and job markets, more and more companies turn to contract work positions. The length of a contract can vary from three to six months, one to two years, or even longer. Although contract work jobs may not come with all the usual perks or benefits (health and dental plans, retirement contributions, etc.), they do provide a regular paycheque and some amount of flexibility. After finishing the contract, you have gained more experience, hopefully have a new work reference or two, made new professional connections with co-workers, and are free to look for and accept other contract work. Or, if the company really liked you and your work, they may extend the contract term or offer you a permanent part-time or full-time position. All around, it can be a win-win situation in providing you with more income-earning choices.

Some consultants may have started out as employees working for a company (or companies) for several years where they gained valuable professional experience and expertise and made professional contacts along the way. This would be the way to establish yourself in your field before making the change or transition to be a consultant.

Being a consultant can offer some flexibility in hours but depending on circumstances which can range from the local or national economic environment to competition from others in the same field, it can take some time to establish yourself as an advisor with regular work and a regular paycheque coming in. If you are thinking about working from home in this capacity, make sure that you take the time to plan in advance the steps you will take — professionally and financially — to be successful.

Working as a consultant can be a great fit for parents who want to stay at home with their children but want to continue having an income and use their education and profession-al experience. It can also work well for those who are retire-ment age and are ready to finish working full-time but want to be semi-retired so that they can interact with people, keep busy, and supplement their retirement income.

> "Working as a consultant can be a great fit for parents who want to stay at home with their children but want to continue having an income and use their education and professional experience."

Contract work could also be the perfect blend between

online, home-based work, and working in an office space outside of the home. You can have the option of working on the contract from home, you can work at the company's office location for the duration of the contract, or maybe a combination of both can be made to work. Working on contract can provide more interaction and contact with others which can be a great fit for those who are more social and outgoing.

Some people who work from home have work that encompasses areas in each of online work, home-based business, and contract work. This can keep work interesting and provides a better chance of having a stable and regular flow of income.

Seven different types of working from home is a lot of information to take in. From where you are at now and based on what your plans and goals are for the future, you will know which one or more of these types of working from home are best suited to you and your plans.

The need to interact with others is a natural part of everyone's life and is part of the considerations about deciding to work from home. It is up to you to determine the degree and amount of interaction you need with others to meet your social needs to lead and live a healthy, properly balanced life for your mental, emotional, and physical health and well-being.

Legal Structure Options

The first option is that of sole proprietorship which means that you are the sole owner and are personally held liable for everything that happens. As a sole proprietor, you can work as a freelancer, finding and submitting work as you go, or on contract, working for another company for a predetermined length of time. Sole proprietorship is simpler and more straightforward than an incorporation. With this form of a working from home structure, you can make decisions that best suit your working needs and consult with outside help, resources, and professionals when needed.

If you decide to incorporate your work-from-home business for reasons pertaining to property, tax, legal liabilities, insurance, or future growth considerations, you have the option of going solo to be your incorporated business's only owner and be responsible for making all the decisions while hiring or contracting consultants and workers as needed. It can take a lot of energy, support, and encouragement to start and run a business even if at the beginning it only makes $10,000 to $15,000 a year. However, you will know the ins and outs of the business forward and backward which can be an advantage. For an incorporated company, take into consideration future steps to prepare for potentially selling or transferring the company to another owner down the road.

Alternately, you may prefer a partnership to start, build, and grow the business with the help and support of a business partner. Even by having a business partner, you will be kept busy working on the day-to-day operations of your business as you build it from the ground up but if your strengths, weaknesses, and personalities complement each other, you will have each other's perspective for making decisions best suited to your work-from-home business. Your business partner may live in the same city as you — or may be located in a different city — and maybe you meet once a week in-person or twice a week through Skype to go over business and other work details.

Working on your own from home, either as a sole proprietor working as a freelancer or on contracts, owner of an incorporated company, or with a business partner, is a decision to make after considering short- and long-term goals; weighing legal, tax, insurance and other liabilities and requirements; doing some market research into the feasibility of your idea; and consulting the input and advice of family, friends, and mentors. Do not rush into anything but instead take your time to think and ponder before making a final decision.

Which form of working from home you ultimately adopt

is up to you and is unique to each person for a variety of reasons and circumstances. Make sure you weigh the information carefully and think about your options and preferences to work on your own or if you prefer or have an opportunity to have a business partner or consult other professionals when necessary.

Takeaway Tips

There are at least seven different types of working from home options to consider and choose from...

1) The preparation and selling of food-based items or products made in-home but sold in stores
2) Services provided at home to customers who come to a home office or studio e.g., dayhome operator, accountant, music or art teacher, hairdresser, massage therapist, yoga instructor, etc.
3) Services, information, or products provided entirely online
4) Businesses which hire contractors on their behalf (different from employees) to work on projects or other work as required
5) Businesses which hire employees who then, in turn, contact prospective clients with the goal of bringing business in
6) Employees who work from home for a business
7) Consultants who work on contract for universities, corporations, etc. from home

Possibilities for the legal structure of your work-from-home business include...

- Sole proprietor
  - Freelancer
  - Contractor
  - Business owner

- Partnership
  - Business owner
  - Partners
- Corporation
  - Business owner
  - Partners

A Team Effort:
Your Work Hours, Working
Goals, and More

In this chapter, lifestyle adjustments, your goals, and more will be addressed to give you the best understanding of how to make the most of your working and resting hours. Putting your energy and focus on a task at a time when you work best is one of the secrets to success. Having all the information on the work-from-home lifestyle will assist you in making the decision that is perfect for your unique situation.

Work Rhythm Flow

When are you the most productive? Do you like to work on many projects at the same time or do you prefer to concentrate just on one task at a time? Do you work most efficiently early in the morning? Or late at night? Or somewhere in between? If you already know the answer to this, power to you! If not, get started figuring out the answer so that you can harness your best hours of the day into being most productive at your job.

Do you work best when it is quiet at home, i.e. before everyone is up or after everyone has gone to bed? Do you focus better and get more done when there is lots going on at home in the background, such as people talking, the phone ringing, people coming in and out

> "Identifying the time of day or night when you are fully focused, and the type of environment which is most conducive to your having the energy to get tasks done, can lead to shorter work hours."

of the house, etc.? Identifying the time of day or night when you are fully focused, and the type of environment which is most conducive to your having the energy to get tasks done, can lead to shorter work hours. You will be more efficient with using your time to complete projects, thus being more productive. And you will be happier that you have that extra time away from business to spend with family and friends, on hobbies and interests, being active outdoors, or giving back to your community.

When considering the hours when you work best, take into account the type of work, job, or project you are going to be doing along with the responsibilities and business tasks required. For example, if part of your tasks includes making calls in the morning but you find that you are most focused in the early afternoon hours, what are the ways that you can motivate yourself to do responsibilities when they need to be done? Can you turn it into a positive by getting the most difficult task done first thing in the day? Would taking a short break every half hour provide the needed energy to see you through a challenging objective?

Another way to make the work rhythm flow work for you is to work in tandem with the weather and seasons. During the summer, you may want to work when it is hottest outside. During the winter, your preference may be to work early in the morning and at night when it is dark outside. Give this a try to learn how the seasons affect your work performance and productivity.

John Ivanko and Lisa Kivirist, authors of *ECOpreneuring: Putting Purpose and the Planet before Profits*, have an excellent section in their book on Biorhythm Balance found on page 190 with some of it shared here:

"If you could only work three hours a day, which three hours would be your "Most Productive Time," your MPT? Everyone proffers a different perspective on this; don't be shy to think out of normal work hour boundaries. Lisa's MPT is 5 am to 8 am. An obvious morning person, she's learned that by tackling a priority project during the first three focused hours in the morning, before Liam wakes and the phone starts ringing, she sets a positive momentum to her whole day.

If you're coming from an office environment, three hours probably doesn't seem like much. "I'm at the office closer to 12 hours a day," you say. But when you eliminate distractions, the office social scene, commuting time, latte runs and administrative meetings, how much of that time is truly productive? By focusing on your best, most creative and prolific productive time block, you open up your daily schedule to other possibilities, like training for a triathlon or just maintaining a regular workout routine at the gym... Working with — not against — your biorhythms naturally takes on a seasonal ebb and flow.

Granted, we live on a farm where seasonal living is embedded in our business and daily routines...But you don't need to live rural to appreciate the seasonal changes. Mother Nature provides us with an annual cyclical flow of themes that we can all tap into. Think of each season as a fresh chapter ushering in new opportunities to connect to the Earth thematically. By listening to these biorhythms, we grow to know ourselves better and can fine-tune our focus. We garner deeper understanding of how we work, create and innovate."

~ From *ECOpreneuring: Putting Purpose and the Planet before Profits* by John Ivanko and Lisa Kivirist.

Using your internal clock in determining your best working hours will help you feel more energized and rested. You will find that you are harnessing your strength of concentration at its peak and to your advantage.

If your choice is to work from home for a company, the likelihood is higher that you will be working regular hours set either by the company or your manager. However, at some point during the interview, offer for employment, or a few months after working on the job, speak up and ask if you can start work at 7 a.m. instead of 9 a.m. or finish at 8 p.m. rather than 5 p.m. (this can work well if colleagues work in different time zones to align start or finish times, if realistic, or collaborate more on work if needed). Starting work earlier in the day means that you can have time in the afternoon to pick up kids from school and enjoy a relaxed and stress-free dinner hour.

Finishing work later in the day means that the morning is yours to devote to having breakfast without rushing, getting the kids to school, and doing errands when lineups at the checkout are shorter.

The Possibilities

In choosing to work from home, one of the greatest advantages is the many available options. You can take it and run with it as far as you want and see where your goals will take you. The only limit is you and what you want to achieve.

Do you want to be a manager? Take on responsibility at work in your current position, learn as much as you can through on-the-job training and professional development, and apply for managerial roles. Even in working from home, the position of a manager is just as important and found just as often as in brick-and-mortar offices.

Is your vision to be making passive income while you employ others to work from home for your company? The possibilities seem endless, especially with technology helping to open so many doors and paths — you could start a company and employ people to work in sales or public relations, just to name a few. Do your research and planning right, and you could find yourself as the CEO of your own company while employing others to work remotely on the marketing, sales, product development, customer service, and business development to grow the profits of your company. Or you can invest in and rent out residential and commercial real estate — apartments, townhomes, houses, stores, shops and land — to generate passive income. Other options are to be a writer, a coach, a consultant to individuals and corporations, or develop and maintain a profitable web-based business. You can also host workshops, retreats, and webinars — either locally, at special locations, or virtually — to teach others how to do something similar to what you are doing, love doing, and have found success in doing.

As you can see, the possibilities and options are many. But the first step is to set goals at least every few months so that you keep on taking small steps to reach your big goals. In setting goals, make sure that they are:

- Measurable so that you can see progress to encourage you along the way;
- Attainable so that they are realistic and you can reach them rather than becoming discouraged; and
- Accountable in that there is someone you can check in with who will give you an objective feedback and cheer you on.

The important process here is to:

1) Set goals
2) Take action on reaching those goals

3) Enlist the support and encouragement (and feedback, as needed) of family and friends, and

4) Revisit and set new goals to progress to where you want to get to.

Do not be impatient when the going is slow (easier said than done sometimes) but try to enjoy the process, see the progress you have made, and figure out ways to work smarter and more efficiently to get closer to your goals.

Government Rules and Regulations

A drawback to working from home can be the seemingly long list of government rules and regulations for business and corporate structure, business law, taxes, etc. These can be a burden and therefore, an obstacle and discouragement by taking up your time, money, and energy resources in starting to work from home. Some regulations, especially related to food, health, and safety standards, are absolutely essential and required to ensure the health and safety of everyone including customers, employees, and others.

If government regulation and bureaucracy are getting in the way of your being able to successfully work from home, then take some action. Contact your municipal, provincial/state, and federal government representative to ask them about resources available to assist you in getting started, or let them know the changes which need to be made based on the difficulties that you have encountered. Sometimes the best solution might be to run for office yourself to make the needed change.

Team of Professionals

In working from home, it is also important to have a team of professionals — accountant, insurance agent/company, computer specialist, lawyer, doctor, dentist, carpenter or handyman, and auto mechanic — around you whom you trust, whom you can ask for professional advice, and who can explain to you the benefits and drawbacks of various business options available to you. Having this group of professionals in place will help ensure that your health, home, business, and work keep running smoothly and in good order and that details or options are not overlooked.

> "It is important to have a team of professionals around you whom you trust, whom you can ask for professional advice, and who can explain to you the benefits and drawbacks of various business options available to you."

Yes, there are many lifestyle considerations to the topic of working from home and some of these presented here may very well affect your decision one way or the other. Your responsibility is to discern which of these considerations fit with your personality, family, and work situation, and goals.

Takeaway Tips

To take the best chance of making remote work a success, identify...

- ✓ When you work best and when you are the most productive — in the morning, afternoon, or evening
- ✓ The possibilities in working from home — some of those are whether you want to grow your business and hire others to work virtually for your business or be a manager for a company
- ✓ Any government rules or regulations you need to be in compliance with as needed

✓ Having a team of professionals — accountant, lawyer, doctor, and others — in place.

Marketing and Finances

There are many books, talks, videos, online resources, and more which cover marketing and finance strategies in-depth. And if you have your own work-from-home business or have published a book, then you will want to have some marketing and financial plan in place to reach customers and followers and make informed financial decisions. You will also want to set aside some time on a regular basis to not only maintain but also review, grow, and change your marketing and financial efforts as needed.

With that being said, I will first share my thoughts on and approaches to marketing.

Marketing

Whether you have a home-based business, brand, or both, it is important to have a good idea of what your marketing focus is for different areas such as short-term, long-term, sales, and community. For myself, at present, the below factors play an important part when I consider, decide on, and act on any aspect of marketing:
- Creativity
- Partnership/Collaboration and Promotion
- Quality of Post
- Quality of Interaction
- Budget

Creativity

In my marketing efforts, I try to come up with creative, outside-the-box ways and approaches to reach, connect, and interact with followers. Sometimes, I have several creative and fun ideas to implement while in other weeks I take longer to come up with or have fewer new marketing concepts surface. However, I strive to learn what is helpful and to stay open to making changes as necessary which leads to creative implementations in marketing. Later in this chapter, I will share the various marketing channels I have tried myself or assisted others with in their business.

Partnership/Collaboration and Promotion

I like to reach out to and get to know other people which is why marketing partnerships or collaborations are a natural part of my marketing focus and path. For example, by searching and learning more about working from home, I have come across several websites on the topic. After looking through the websites, I reached out through contact forms or by email to some of the people who ran the online sites. Some responded by inviting me to write a post which they would share on their blog and website and in exchange, I would share their website and social media links on my website and social media channels. This resulted in both parties increasing their audience reach and gaining new followers or customers. It has been a fun way of getting to know others who enjoy remote work while at the same time sharing some of my passion and knowledge with them, too, thus resulting in collaboration and cross promotion.

Including marketing partnership in your marketing strategy means that you will be able to have your information — name, brand, company, and product or service — spread to a wider audience. By using a variety of means, your information can be shared on others' websites, social media (Facebook, blog,

Twitter, Instagram, Pinterest, YouTube), and e-newsletter channels through:

- Direct links back to your website or social media
- Interviews with you about your expertise, what you do, and the service(s) or product(s) you offer
- Reviews of your product or service
- Guest blog posts
- Writing regular content such as an article

As an example, if you have a business which builds and provides greenhouses, you could reach out — by e-mail, phone, or attending an in-person trade event — to another business which provides landscaping services. You would ask if that business would share your website link on their social media channels or let you write a guest post on greenhouses for their blog and website if you would do the same in exchange for their business. In this way, you reach their audience and they reach your audience in related fields, thus resulting in both businesses potentially doubling or tripling their reach.

If you have an idea for a marketing partnership or promotion, or someone else reaches out to you with a suggestion for one, give it some thought to see if it is an approach that could be beneficial for you and help you achieve your goals. If the partnership or promotion seems like a good fit, get started on implementing it as soon as you can.

Quality of Post

When I post on social media platforms or write something for my e-newsletter, my focus is on the quality of what I am sharing with followers. By quality, I mean content which is of value or has a benefit to the reader. This could mean that the content of the post contains:

- Something educational or informative for followers to learn from such as announcing a writing contest or introducing a new technique or offering a sale or a course;

- Something encouraging or inspirational such as a quote, a success story on working from home, or a resource that may be helpful; or
- Something beautiful and creative such as photos of flowers placed on a desk in a home office and before-and-after photos of a remodelled, renovated, and redecorated home office.

When I post or share content on my platforms, my intention and goal is to provide quality content — informative, thoughtful, encouraging, beautiful, and creative — which followers learn from, enjoy, and look forward to.

Quality of Interaction

Creating valuable interactions with my followers is also a key part in how I view and determine the success of my marketing and platform. Quality interaction results from the high quality of posting. Because my followers know that I choose to post content which is also of benefit to them and is worth their taking the time to read and engage with, they are more likely to interact by posting a comment, liking, or retweeting. I show my appreciation for their interaction by thanking them for their observation and replying to their comment. Or, if they have shared a tip or photo which I think others would like and learn from, then I share it on my platform(s).

Marketing Budget

In any marketing plan, it is important to take into account and make decisions based on your budget. If you have a smaller budget to work with, you may have to be more creative in thinking of available options and ways to reach your target demographic and audience. However much of a marketing budget you have, you may like to combine both tried-and-true methods along with trying new avenues to engage with your followers and clients or customers. Another way of assessing the value of marketing is the cost of reaching individual potential customers through micro-targeting and the resulting sales.

As it may be of interest to readers, below is a list (arranged by group) of the various marketing initiatives I have tried and used over the years as a writer/author and small business owner and also have assisted other small businesses with their marketing plans:

Social Media	Website Platforms	Online Events
- Facebook	- Wix	- Zoom
- Twitter	- WordPress	- Guest on
- Pinterest		others' podcasts

E-newsletter	Virtual Classifieds
- Mailchimp	- Kijiji
- Constant Contact	

Direct Marketing
- Lawn signs
- Cold-calling
- Micro-marketing
- Hand-delivering flyers door-to-door
- Tables/booths at events, fairs, markets, and other venues
- Writing articles and stories for magazines, newspapers, and online publications

While you think about and develop your own marketing plan and strategy, make sure to consider what is important to you and your brand. Is it the number of followers? Is it dependent on which social media platforms you are going to be on? Is it the frequency and the kind and quality of your post? Does your marketing plan include a budget and if yes, how much is feasible to spend each month, quarter, or year and on what? Answering these questions, while at the same time being flexible in trying new ways of reaching and connecting with your audience, can provide a good start and foundation to your marketing endeavors.

> "While you think about and develop your own marketing plan and strategy, make sure to consider what is important to you and your brand."

Finances

What I share below on finances is by no means meant to be a complete, comprehensive, or professional advice. Rather, its purpose and intent are to encourage you to look at your current financial circumstances to see where you are at now and make any necessary adjustments in the direction you are going and wanting to be.

Have a Budget – Business and Personal

This is a must so that you would know where your money goes and so that you can track on what and how much money you are spending. You can adjust and spend more or less in given categories, particularly variable expenses (Entertainment, Travel, Food – Personal, Marketing – Business), each month as long as your expenses are less than your income. Without a budget, it will be much harder to stay on track financially or even to reach financial goals.

There are several tools you can utilize to create a budget

and track your spending. You can either find an online program to use, you can use an Excel spreadsheet, or you can even use a piece of paper or notebook to track your spending habits and create a budget.

Financial Goals

What are your financial goals? Do you want to pay off your mortgage as soon as possible? Do you want to buy your first home? Or maybe your goal is to buy an investment property and generate rental income or purchase a business and make a profit?

Whatever your goals are, write them down so that you know what you are working toward. Then, it will help you stay on track with your budget and anything extra that you make can be directed to getting you closer to your financial goals.

Banking and Fees

Choose a financial institution and a banking plan which works for your finances as well as for your short- and long-term financial and business goals. Make sure to consider whether you need a business account in addition to a personal account and if yes, whether you want to have both at the same financial institution or not. Check your bank account and credit card balances at least once a week to ensure that every transaction and amount have been recorded properly and that there are no unauthorized entries.

Finally, make it a point to understand and know all of the fees and interest charges which you are being billed for and are paying for. Examples of fees and interest include — but are not limited to — monthly bank plan fee, credit card interest, credit card balance insurance, non-sufficient funds (NSF) fee, and more.

Scaling Up

If you are starting your own home-based, remote business, take a few moments to give some thought to whether you plan to grow, expand, and streamline your business. If this is the direction that you are going in, set aside some time to consider what steps you may need to take in the future. Some examples include:

- Will you need a virtual assistant at some point who will complete various administrative tasks, leaving you to focus on doing what needs to be done to grow the business?
- If you begin doing business internationally, how will you convert and accept payment from different currencies?
- What kind of personal and business insurance will you require if your business grows?
- Will you need to upgrade or make changes to your branding and online presence – logo, website, social media, etc.?
- Might you need to outsource some of the work, such as to hire freelancers for a project or on contract, or maybe even hire one, two, or more employees to manage the workload from increased business?

Being aware of the above situations you may encounter in the future can help you begin to think about and plan for solutions in the present.

Saving

Put money aside into savings, an emergency fund, and retirement. As soon as you get money, put it into these separate accounts before you spend it. Setting up automatic transfers to your savings, emergency fund, and retirement accounts can make it easy to ensure that it happens on a regular basis. You can also set money aside to save for things such as a vacation each year, a new laptop/camera, or anything which may cost more to purchase — a vehicle, home or other property, or new appliance. They should be items that you know you will need to buy or acquire down the road.

Diversify Your Income

Having several sources of income, or working toward making that happen, is an important part of success in working from home and remote work. Many people who work from home, including some of those who were interviewed for this book (see **Part 2: Extraordinary People Who Work from Home**), agree with this and have put this approach into practice. With economic uncertainties and the possibility of pandemics or other changes beyond one's control, it is important now more than ever before to diversify your income.

Why is having diverse sources of income important? Because if one or two sources of income slow down or stop completely, you will still have one, two or more income streams coming in. Having more than one or even two different sources of income can also help you be less stressed, both short- and long-term, about your finances and let you weather and make it through lean times better.

"Having more than one or even two different sources of income can also help you be less stressed, both short- and long-term, about your finances and let you weather and make it through lean times better."

Diversifying your income may require some creativity in thinking up and implementing ways to do so. Having income sources from a combination of both online pursuits and in-person work is also smart. Create passive income streams by selling items online which people can buy anytime:

- Books	- Webinars	- Video tutorials
- E-books	- Downloads	- Membership sites
- Coaching	- Online courses	

Make money through a hands-on skill that you can teach or a product that you can make for others:

- Woodworking
- Farming (crops, animals, flowers)
- Permaculture
- Gardening (fruits, vegetables, plants, flowers)
- Beekeeping
- Baking (breads, pies, desserts, cookies, muffins)
- Pets (dogs, cats, horses, cows, pigs, chickens)
- Handiwork (knitting, sewing, crocheting, alterations)
- Music instruction (teaching an instrument or voice, music theory, recording)
- Or other skills that you have and that you may want to share which others would be interested to acquire

In addition to working from home, consider working part-time or seasonally outside the home such as at a:

- Bookstore
- Coffee or tea shop
- Post office
- Grocery store
- Garden/nursery centre
- Healthcare centre
- Bed & Breakfast
- Farm (urban or rural)
- Or other local service or business

Living Debt-Free

If you have debt — outstanding credit card balances, mortgage, line of credit, student loans, car loans, loans to family or friends — then that means that you owe money to the bank or others and are paying interest on those outstanding amounts.

Do you know how much you are paying in interest each month in addition to the monthly debt payments? If you do not know the amount of interest you are paying each month, then the figure will probably surprise you, particularly if you owe money on several cards.

Start by paying off the highest interest rate loan(s) first and continue from there. Once you pay off one loan, take the amount you were paying on it and put it toward the next loan, thereby shortening the time needed to pay off the next loan. Make sure to pay off all your loans as quickly as you can. It will give you a wonderful feeling of freedom.

Giving Back

Remember to include giving back as a regular part of your budget. Giving back to your local community, favorite charities, and other causes and organizations can be something to look forward to and enjoy. Knowing that you are helping and making a positive difference is a feeling like no other.

What Is Important to You?

The answer to this question will depend on a combination of your age and stage in life as well as your financial goals. If more hours are needed at the beginning as you start your business, find a way to look after your health by building in activities and time to reduce stress such as holistic care and relaxation rituals.

Or is it more important to you in the present to have a remote job working for a company which offers benefits such as a retirement matching program, health benefits, and two to three weeks of vacation a year but with less flexibility over your schedule? This is something which you need to think about. Only you have the answer to this as you know what your present circumstances — family, financial, health, and work — are along with what your goals are for the future and what you need to do to accomplish those goals.

Wills, Trusts and Other Important Documents

Do you have a will or trust in place in the event of your death? How about a Personal Directive and Enduring Power of Attorney? Whether you become seriously ill or in the event of your death, these are important documents to have in place. Look into the documents required and the tax implications of each in your country. For Canadian readers, a good source of information is *The Canadian Guide to Will and Estate Planning: Everything You Need to Know Today to Protect Your Wealth and Your Family Tomorrow* by Douglas Gray and John Budd. For readers who are U.S. citizens, financial expert Suze Orman has lots of great advice about setting up wills and trusts and their tax implications along with having a Personal Directive and Enduring Power of Attorney.

It is also important to check that you have enough coverage as well as the right policies in the fields of life insurance and health insurance. There are several available options, so learn about insurance coverage in your area and which ones meet your current needs and future requirements.

Your Team

It is important to assemble a financial team with professionals whom you trust to give you sound advice. The professionals you will want on your team are:

- An accountant
- A life insurance advisor
- A business lawyer
- A health insurance advisor
- A will & estates lawyer
- An investment advisor/financial advisor

If you are looking for any of the above professionals to add to your financial team, ask for referrals and recommendations either from other professionals already on your team, from members of your business community, or from customer reviews.

You can also ask friends or do an online search to learn who has given good service. Review your finances and goals with each professional on your team on a regular basis, whenever you have questions, and whenever there is a change in your circumstances (a change to your income or business, a new child in your family, house move, etc.).

Resources

Here are some suggested resources, which I have found to be of value, for you to consider looking at if you want to learn more about how to plan for the future with the money you make:

- *The 9 Steps to Financial Freedom: Practical and Spiritual Steps So You Can Stop Worrying* by Suze Orman
- *The Retirement Guide for 50+: Winning Strategies to Make Your Money Last a Lifetime* by Suze Orman
- Suze Orman's Personal Financial Online Course
- *Biblical Economics: A Commonsense Guide to Our Daily Bread* by R.C. Sproul Jr.
- *More Than Finances: A Design for Freedom* by Larry Burkett
- *Rich Dad, Poor Dad* by Robert Kiyosaki
- *The Rules of Wealth: A Personal Code for Prosperity and Plenty* by Richard Templar
- *The Canadian Guide to Will and Estate Planning: Everything You Need to Know Today to Protect Your Wealth and Your Family Tomorrow* by Douglas Gray and John Budd
- *Stop Working: Here's How You Can!* by Derek Foster
- *Stop Working Too: You Still Can!* by Derek Foster

Takeaway Tips

When creating and implementing your marketing plan, consider elements such as...

- ✓ Creativity
- ✓ Partnership/Collaboration and Promotion
- ✓ Quality of Post
- ✓ Quality of Interaction
- ✓ Marketing Budget

As you take a look at your finances and set financial goals, keep in mind that it is important to...

- Have a budget
- Set financial goals
- Consider banking fees and interest charges
- Think about scaling up
- Put money aside into savings, emergency fund, and retirement account
- Live debt-free
- Give back
- Know what is important to you
- Prepare your will, trust documents and other important letters
- Have a financial team in place
- Access book and web resources when needed

The Inspiring Home Office

Every work-from-home space needs to have the essentials: the right room and amount of space to work in, good lighting, the proper chair, the right desk, and adequate desk space. Having the best of the essentials will help you concentrate on and produce your best work, keep you organized, and make you want to be at your work desk each day. Even more than the essentials, though, your work space also needs to be a special place which you look forward to working in and which holds touches of your personality.

> "Having the best of the essentials will help you concentrate on and produce your best work, keep you organized, and make you want to be at your work desk each day."

First, we will talk about each one of the essential items that will make your nook a functional, efficient place to get work done each day.

Essentials
The Right Room and Amount of Space

The physical location of your work space at home can have a direct and significant impact on both your productivity and quality of work. Because floorplans vary from home to home and because everyone has a unique vision and different needs for what their work space should look like and entail, no two home offices will be alike.

What should you take into consideration in selecting the right room and amount of space to be able to work in? Start by answering these questions:

- Do you need a door or wall to separate your work space? There are a few reasons why this might be needed. If the phone calls you make for work need to be kept private or confidential, this can be one reason to keep a separate work space.
- Do you need to minimize interruptions and distractions coming from family or the rest of the home (seeing the laundry piling up and waiting to be done, watching the bills that need to be paid stacking up, etc.)? Remember, work needs to be done and done on time, too. For a separate work space at home, a den or other similar space could be the solution.

If having a room, as a completely separate work space, is not going to happen, then choose a corner of a room such as in the living room or dining room (you can have a work space in your bedroom but keep electronics out of the space so that your bedroom is a place for true rest and relaxation). If you can fit all your files and necessary supplies for getting work done into the corner of a room, then even though it may seem small, you may still have the right amount of space to get work done. You can always have a bookshelf in a different part of your home where you keep other books, materials, and supplies you may need to reference from time to time but do not neces-sarily require on a day-to-day basis.

Picking a room or corner of a room for a work space at home may require some creativity to make it work. It could mean rearranging or moving furniture around for a better layout, choosing furniture which serves two purposes such as both as a desk and storage space, or perhaps doing some small renovations such as moving or taking down a wall to open up a large space, moving or adding a window, or making two rooms instead of one. Whatever the change(s) needed to be made, the goal is to have the area become your happy place to go to work in.

Good Lighting

Two forms of good lighting are needed. The first is natural lighting which, through a good-sized window(s), allows you to look out and notice what the weather is like, see the nature in your yard, or watch the comings and goings in your neighborhood. Plus, seeing the sunshine streaming in and perhaps warming up your office space can be a great pick-me-up on days that may hold discouragement, disappointment, or a setback.

The second form of lighting is from artificial indoor lighting such as floor or desk lamps, track lights, pot lights, chandeliers, or some other ceiling light. A table or floor lamp, suited to the height of your desk and set to the correct angle for best lighting, provides a suitable light for seeing information clearly on papers or on the computer screen without tiring your eyes.

Hard Wire Your Work Area

Ensure that your space is hard wired with at least one wall plug-in for both an ethernet (internet) cable and phone jack. If you have the option of having two each of these wall plug-ins, then it will give you more choice in where you can have your computer and landline phone and how you arrange your office furniture. By hard wiring your office area, you can turn off Wi-Fi on your computer and mobile phone, thereby helping to reduce electromagnetic frequencies (EMFs) where you work (for more information on the effects of EMFs, read the textbox at the end of the *Healthy Home, Healthy You* chapter).

Proper Chair/Seat

Selecting the right type of chair is paramount to your comfort when working from home. Things to consider in selecting your chair include the material the chair is made of (whether it is made from wood or leather, whether it is already padded or not, etc.), the height adjustability, the softness or firmness of the seat padding, and the mobility of the chair (ex: does it have wheels for easy moving, is it easy to fold up for storage and saving space, etc.). Having a back rest as part of the chair can be a good idea for being able to lean back, to stretch or to rest, and change your seating position from time to time. If the chair is not padded, you can add a small pillow to soften the chair seat.

You do not necessarily need to buy a new chair just for your work space. Perhaps a chair that you already have, like one found in the kitchen eating area, can serve a dual purpose. This could save you space which can be especially helpful if your home has a small square footage.

Desk

Does your desk allow you the versatility of either standing or sitting while working? Having the choice of alternating between standing and sitting as you work keeps you more focused on tasks and is healthier for you as you can change positions. There are two options here: one is to be able to adjust the height of your desk to go from sitting to standing (think *Varidesk* which is a company that makes desks allowing to change between sitting and standing) and the other is to have a desk height which allows you to stand at it or sit if the height of the chair is right (such as having a bar-style chair or stool). Or you may use a small box underneath your computer to raise it just enough for a comfortable standing position.

What material do you want your desk to be made from — all natural as in light-colored pine wood or a dark oak wood or some other natural material? How about color — a dark stain or all white or a modern look of steel and glass? Does the desk fold up for easy storage or does it have various desk space sizes that you can shorten and lengthen, by adding an extension, depending on how much space you need for your computer and for working? Consider these questions and your answers to them as you select the desk that is best suited to you, your work, and your space.

Desk Space

Having enough room on your desk for papers, office supplies, a computer, and a phone will make working from home more enjoyable. Think about how much desk space you will need both to complete work and leave your work in place to come back to during your next working hours. Does your work require lots of space for papers, folders, and binders or does your work need enough desk area to have space for two computers? Nothing can be more frustrating than constantly having to put away work and then take it out again the next day. Important papers and other important materials can get lost or misfiled through constant moving, besides wasting time before starting work.

Storage

Do you have lots of papers and files which you need for work? Take a look at the available storage options which come with the desk that you are considering acquiring for your work from home. Are there drawers and dividers for placement of papers to keep things organized and separated? Is there enough room on the desk that you can you add your own surface or standing storage options suited to your personal style? Or perhaps a separate filing cabinet which can fit under your desk or in a corner of your work space is the best solution. Make sure to give storage solutions some thought now so that when you start your work, you have a place for everything and everything in its place.

Robyn, a former music student of mine and now my friend, who works in the oil and gas industry, had to transition to working from home at the request of her employer. She added creatively to her storage space by making use of a music stand to hold workbooks, papers, and sticky notes.

Robyn, a former music student of mine and now my friend, added creatively to her available storage space by making use of a music stand to hold workbooks, papers, and sticky notes.
Photo by Robyn.

In addressing storage issues, make sure to also make the best of what you already have at home, as the above photo illustrates. You may be surprised at the many ways that some items can be used. To make your space a truly unique and inspiring place to work from, add these for a touch of life, color, and personality.

Personalize with Personality
Plants

Plants add greenery to a space and bring some of the outdoors in. If you live in a northern climate with lots of snow or a climate with lots of rain during the colder months, having a green plant will brighten up your space and remind you that spring and summer will return soon. Plants are also good for cleaning the indoor air of toxins and purifying the air. Some favorite and popular indoor plants are:

- Ivy
- Cactus
- Pothos
- Jade
- Kalancho
- Peace Lily
- Aloe
- Philodendron
- Spider Plant
- Boston Fern
- Chrysanthemum
- Weeping Fig

Choose a plant with sunlight and watering requirements that will work for you and enjoy your new little green friend. Whenever you feel the need to see some greenery and something lovely to look at, it will be right there in front of you to view and enjoy. To learn more about the benefits of house plants, a recommended read is the section on houseplants in Michelle Polk's *Healing Houseplants: How to Keep Plants Indoors for Clean Air, Healthier Skin, Improved Focus, and a Happier Life!*

Flowers

In addition to plants, treat your office space to flowers. Leave a little space on your desk, on a windowsill in front or to the side of your work area, or somewhere else close by for a vase filled with a beautiful bouquet of flowers. Whether you select a vase that has been in your family for a few generations, a vase with a modern cut, or a colorful vase, the vase can also communicate something about your style.

Buy a bouquet of flowers or just a single showpiece like a gerbera once a month, or more often if it works for you and your budget, just to add a fun splash of color to your home office. Fresh flowers can provide an extra touch of beauty to the space and lift your mood, making your whole day that much better. Or consider a seasonal arrangement to add to the décor of your work space. Whether it is tulips, roses, mums, sunflowers, gerberas, or some combination with filler plants added in, get flowers which will add sunshine and joy to your home office.

Artwork

Any size of artwork, small or large and short or tall, to add to your work from home office will give it a touch of color, expression, creativity, enjoyment, and a space to look forward to. You may decide to showcase any subject matter you may like such as a dreamy landscape, an interesting portrait, a colorful cityscape, or a calming still life. Or, you can choose a drawing drawn in pencil, pen or ink, or pastel. Perhaps even a bronze sculpture or a wood or soapstone carving might fit into your space.

To make the artwork in your home office even more special and meaningful to you, you may want to display artwork which has been a treasured family item or perhaps a painting which was given to you by a family member on a special occasion in your life such as graduation or wedding.

Color

A bright splash of color can do wonders for creating an inspiring space to work in. Adding some color to your home office can be done in several ways. One way is to paint one wall with an accent color, such as choosing to paint one wall blue or yellow while the other walls are painted white. Another idea is to paint stripes along one wall and yet another idea would be to paint a mural or a stencil design on a wall or two.

Color can also be added in the form of curtains, valances, chair cushions, ribbons, stuffed animals, or a tiny carpet to rest your feet on. By including some color in your home office, you will make the space come alive and add a dash of your own personality.

Inspirational Sayings

If you have favorite inspirational quotes from motivational speakers or other texts, set them up where you can see them. Frame these inspirational sayings and then display them on your desk or hang them on a wall that you can see when you are working at your desk. Seeing and reading the quotes on a daily basis can help motivate, encourage, and remind you about why you are working from home and help you reach your goals. Inspirational sayings can keep you focused on your goals and be a great way to celebrate regularly that remote working is one of the best decisions you have made!

Vision Board

A vision board is a board which contains images of various aspects of your ideal life. Some of these aspects might be:
- Getting and being in shape
- Your family
- Having an organized office space
- Coffee art photos
- What your perfect or ideal home looks like
- Where you want to retire
- Where you want to live in five or ten years
- Your dream home office space
- The amount in your bank account or how much money you want to make each month

By placing your vision board in a spot where you will see it every day, the idea is to be reminded of and encouraged by your goals so that you make the decisions and take the actions to bring your goals to life. Take the time and have fun choosing and placing the images on your board which will inspire you to reach and realize your ideal life. Then, display your vision board in your home office in a location where you will see the images every day.

Maps

If traveling and world destinations are part of what makes you who you are, then add a map to your office space. On your map, you can show the places you have been to or the places you want to visit one day. Or maybe the map can remind you of where your family came from and where family members are located now. You may like to select a map of the world or a map that focuses on just one country or continent. A map can also show time zones which can be helpful to know when scheduling talks and calls.

Maps are available in several different sizes and colors. You can choose to display a framed map or laminated map on a wall in your home office. If you are short on wall space, then a map placemat placed on your desk or a globe to place on a bookshelf or on your desk could be the solution.

Accomplishments

Degrees, diplomas, certificates, trophies, awards, and badges all say a lot about who you are and what you have already done. It says that you have worked hard to learn something, achieved a goal, showed dedication, and have interests, skills, and talents. So be proud of what you have accomplished and proudly display that degree on the wall or that award on the desk. Let it be something that you see every day in your home office. Let it remind you that you can do anything that you put your mind to.

Photos of Loved Ones

Put up a few photos of family and friends in your work space. This will continually inspire you as you see who you are doing this for, why you are doing this (for example, to spend more time with family rather than commute, etc.), and the future goals that you want to reach to make their life easier (ex: be debt-free sooner, have travel money, buy a vacation property, or retire earlier, etc.) by working from home.

Holiday Decorations

For any holidays and special days or events you celebrate, decorate your home office space even if it is just with a single item. That might mean decorations such as:
- Ribbons
- Images
- Wreaths
- Ornaments
- Garlands
- Signs with sayings
- Christmas tree
- Nutcracker

Include the items which will give your work space that holiday touch and feel. Each time there is a special event or holiday, you can change the decorations in your office so that there is always something to look forward to and always new items to decorate with and look at.

Yoga Mat/Exercise Gear

Why not keep your yoga mat and some exercise gear — dumbbells, resistance stretch bands, a medicine ball, or a re-bounder — in your home office? Not only will it say that you prioritize your health and being active but it can also say something about your style and colors that you like. You can keep exercise equipment in a basket and tuck it under your desk or in a corner of your home office. When you have a few minutes free or are taking a break, and if you have a few feet of space nearby, get on your mat or pick up some dumbbells and get moving while also letting go of stress and having fun.

Air Diffuser/Himalayan Salt Lamp

Freshen up the air in your home office by using an air diffuser with essential oils. Some favorite and awesome essential oils to use, and their uses, are:

Relaxation	Energy	Cleaning
Rose	Lemon	Tea Tree
Lavender	Rosemary	Eucalyptus
Bergamot	Peppermint	Lavender
Spearmint	Sweet Orange	Peppermint
Ylang Ylang		

Filling the air with essential oils can help you feel both energized and more relaxed. An excellent resource on essential oils is *Essential Oils Pocket Reference (8th Edition)* published by Life Science (additional books on essential oils are suggested in **Appendix B - Resources**).

A Himalayan salt lamp will provide a lovely warm and inviting glow in your office space which can help in feeling more relaxed, too. If you decide to add one to your space, take the time to choose the lamp with a shape and color that you like. Some Himalayan salt lamps come with a dimmer so that you can choose the level of brightness when the lamp is on.

Seize this opportunity to make your home office space your own. Add your own touch to it so that it is a place that you want to come to work in. Not only should it include the necessary equipment to complete work every day but it also needs to be

> "Seize this opportunity to make your home office space your own. Add your own touch to it. Not only should it include the necessary equipment but it also needs to be a home to your favorite things."

a home to your favorite things and your personality as part of the work area. Whether you have a big or small area to work with, see how creative and fun you can be in the design and decoration of your home office.

Takeaway Tips

As you set up your home office space, keep these essential elements in mind...

✓ Choose the right room and amount of space
✓ Have good lighting
✓ Hard wire your area
✓ Select the proper chair and seat
✓ Have adequate desk space
✓ Ensure there is enough storage

Enjoy making your work space your own by personalizing it with some of these items...

- Plants and flowers
- Artwork
- Color
- Inspirational sayings
- Vision board
- Maps
- Accomplishments
- Photos of loved ones

- Holiday decorations
- Yoga mat/Exercise gear
- Air diffuser/Himalayan salt lamp

Making the Transition from Office to Home Office

Approaching your manager and/or employer to explore the option of working from home can seem like a daunting task, especially if it is something that is new to your company and has not been done or tried before. However, with a little preparation and a strong track record at work of submitting projects on time to meet work deadlines, working well and communicating efficiently with co-workers, and arriving at work a little earlier each day, there is nothing to fear.

Companies have a lot to gain by encouraging and letting their employees find the right balance between working in the office and working from home. For some employees, working from home full-time will work best while for others,

> "Companies have a lot to gain by encouraging and letting their employees find the right balance between working in the office and working from home."

they will be most productive working two or three days from home and the rest of the time working in the office. Organizations which make it known that they support and encourage working from home are seen as being innovative and having a happier and more engaged workforce.

To begin the process of transitioning to working from home, start by setting a time to talk with your employer. Avoid choosing a time when there is a huge project due the next day and everyone in the office, including your employer, is racing against time to meet that deadline. Instead, choose a time when your employer is not busy and things at work are quiet. Then, just before going into the meeting, stand up tall, roll your shoulders back, be confident, and smile.

When you go into the meeting, be prepared. Be ready to explain how you will make working from home work, not only for you but also for the company, in the following areas:

- Communicating with co-workers and managers
- Attending office meetings virtually or coming into the office (i.e., coming to the office for Monday morning meetings to go over tasks and goals for the coming week)
- Contacting and meeting with clients
- The feasibility of working from home full-time, part-time (i.e., two days from home and three days in the office or vice versa) or something in between
- Collaborating with colleagues on projects
- Submitting work virtually or bringing completed work to the office to meet deadlines
- The potential to save the company money by your working from home (if this is the case, make sure you do your research and present the numbers to support this)
- Job sharing with another colleague if it is your intention to switch to working from home part-time (talk about this with your colleague ahead of time before sharing this with your employer in the meeting)

Having answers and solutions ready to the above potential

issues will show your manager and employer that you have given working from home lots of consideration, and that you are ready to minimize and counter any challenges, setbacks, or effects that may occur during the transition period.

During the meeting with your employer, you might like to ask the following questions to make sure that you, the employee, and they, the management/owners, have the same vision of working from home going forward:

- When would working from home start?
- What, if any, challenges does the employer foresee and how can those be mitigated?
- Are there any resources or support that the company can offer (e.g., professional development, remote tech support, help line, etc.)?
- Is there a trial period, say for three months, during which to see how working from home goes and then after that time to evaluate what works well and what can be improved?
- What are the company's short- and long-term goals for employees working from home and how can you be part of the planning or help with it?

Approaching the meeting with your manager, about working from home, with an open mind to their suggestions and ideas is essential. When it comes to transitioning to working from home, it is important to understand that this change may not happen overnight but may take time. Ensure that you and your employer are on the same timeline when it comes to a start date for beginning to work from home.

After getting the approval to work from home, take care to continue to be self-disciplined, start work on time, and finish and submit work before deadlines. Then, after a pre-determined trial period (or sooner if there are indications of communication issues, technical snags, or client comments), have another meeting to evaluate how it is going. Some areas to evaluate

include:
- Frequency of communication with colleagues and if the amount and type of communication method is enough and the best one for collaborating on work
- Frequency of communication/contact with clients and if client queries are being responded to in a timely manner
- Whether quality of work completed and submitted continues to meet and exceed company/client expectations
- Any other changes your manager has noticed or any feedback your manager can provide to help you reach company goals for the quarter, year, etc.
- Changes or improvements to be made to the technology or equipment you are using for working from home

There is plenty to talk about and review after giving working from home a try. Look at it as a learning process that will keep on improving over time. If you are hesitating about talking with your employer about working from home, do not wait any longer. It is possible that some may say no but do not let that discourage you. If you truly want to work from home, either try to be patient until your manager or someone else with authority gives you the go-ahead, search for a new job that allows working from home from the get-go, or start your own business working remotely. There are many options and solutions to make working from home feasible, so do not take no for an answer and if you get a yes, keep on smiling and working hard.

Keeping in Touch with Co-workers

Keep those communication lines open with your co-workers and the same goes for your boss or manager and clients. If you need more information on how best to answer a client's question, pick up the phone or send an e-mail and learn from your co-workers what their approaches and solutions are. You might be surprised when you hear their suggestion as it could be something that you never thought of but just the same, it might be an absolutely brilliant idea. That is where co-workers can make a difference — to give you a helping hand when you need one and you, in turn, will be there to return the help when they need it. It works both ways.

Do you have colleagues who live in the same city or close geographical area as you do? That is great. Why not meet outside of work hours to get to know each other better? It can be a good feeling to build a support system amongst all who work from home for the same company or even have their own business from home. Whether you get together and connect with remote colleagues virtually or in-person, here are some ways to spend time together outside of work:

> "Do you have colleagues who live in the same city or close geographical area as you do? That is great. Why not meet outside of work hours to get to know each other better?"

- Start a book group
- Hold monthly themed dinners
- Organize a monthly hike or ice skate
- Play sports or do an activity like tennis or bowling
- Go on a weekly walk to explore different neighborhoods
- Engage in creative activities such as art, crafts, photography or writing
- Play creative games like *Bananagrams*, *Jobstacles*, or other idea-oriented games

It might be more work to intentionally get to know co-workers who also work remotely compared to colleagues who meet every day in the office but it is worth the effort. If you have had a new colleague join the team recently, include them by inviting them to the get-togethers, too.

At one of my jobs, my colleague Christine and I enjoyed walks, afternoon tea and coffee, and dinners together at a restaurant about once a month.

Colleagues Barbori and Christine enjoying a walk in the fresh air.

Each month, we would try a different cuisine such as Swiss-Italian or Indian. In addition to trying a new restaurant, it was a great time of talking and getting to know each other better. Below, Christine shares her thoughts and experiences on how she gets to know colleagues more outside of work and what she enjoys most about it:

"Something I've always enjoyed about starting a new job is getting the opportunity to meet my colleagues. I have been fortunate to have worked with some amazing, warm-hearted people. When I first started an internship in Dumfries in Scotland, I was so nervous. I was alone in a new country and starting a new job. During my first week, my supervisor invited me to a former colleague's going away party. Simply receiving an invitation to go out made me feel much more at ease in my new workplace. The going away party took place at a fancy restaurant and there were many colleagues from my work there, so it

presented an incredible opportunity to break the ice and get to know them in a relaxed setting. I remember walking to the restaurant with my supervisor, and along the way she pointed out different landmarks, fun stores to visit, and the best places to buy groceries. This simple act of meeting outside of the workplace instantly made me feel at home, and a part of the team. I was also invited to join the whole team at a ghost walk, where actors led a tour through the town of Dumfries and would show us the haunted locations around the town. This was such a fun and unique experience, which really allowed me to further bond with my co-workers.

Every time I went out with my colleagues, I noticed a difference in my attitude when arriving back at work the next day. I felt more confident and secure in my position there, making it easier for me to ask questions and really embrace my new role."

As Christine shares, getting to know your colleagues outside of work can also result in better and increased communication at work. Are you going away on holidays? Now is the time to ask a colleague to cover for you (i.e. answer client questions, phone calls, e-mails, etc.) while you are away rather than a day or two before your scheduled take-off time. Be respectful of your co-workers' time and ask them about vacation cover at least one month in advance if you can (but more months ahead of time is okay too — just remind them a few weeks before that you are going on vacation). Also let them know if there will be any important call or sale coming in during your absence and how they should handle it. Leave notes to help with clients' files, too. Keep in mind that it is a nice gesture to reciprocate. If you find out that a colleague is heading off to a warmer climate to escape the cold and snow, offer to cover for them. It is always nice to have one less thing to remember to do before going on a well-deserved break.

Did one of your co-workers make a big sale, close a deal,

pass an important test, or get promoted? Was it someone's birthday, anniversary, or graduation? Congratulate them on that milestone or event. It took time, hard work, persistence, and perhaps even patience to wait for it to come through and happen. So, send them an e-mail, give them a card, or pick up the phone and give them a call to congratulate them on a job well done. They have earned it.

Remember to stay in contact with your manager. Let them know when you have a question, perhaps about the process of how to properly record a sale, or need clarification to make sure that you understand exactly how they want that document or presentation to be formatted for submission. If something comes up in your schedule and you need to take a morning or afternoon off or instead of working Monday as usual you need to switch and work on Friday, communicate with your boss about these scheduling changes or conflicts with as much advance notice as you can give. Respecting your manager's time, being professional, and ensuring that you will get all your work done and on time will go a long way to making allowances for these accommodations in work hours.

What are some ways to keep in touch with co-workers? The use of Zoom to communicate among virtual teams has increased but there are other platforms which can be used. Phone and e-mail, of course, are two of the many devices you can use to communicate effectively and efficiently with your co-workers and manager. Here are some suggestions for other tools and platforms to use for easy communication:
- Zoom
- Skype
- Slack
- RingCentral
- WebEx
- Workplace by Facebook
- Adobe Connect

- Google Hangout
- Facebook messenger and groups

If your company already has and uses some of the above platforms, keep on using them as they are great tools for communicating. If you feel that your company could try a different platform as it would increase productivity and ease of communication, bring the suggestion to your employer along with the supporting evidence to back up your suggestion.

With the platforms available to connect remotely, it is easier than ever before to keep in touch with your virtual team. Take the time to get to know co-workers to create a welcoming and supportive workplace environment and team.

Takeaway Tips

In making the transition from office to home office, be prepared to address and find solutions to the following with your manager...

- ✓ What, if any, challenges does the employer foresee and how can those be mitigated?
- ✓ What is the proposed timeline for the first day of starting to work from home?
- ✓ Are there any resources or support that the company can offer (e.g., professional development, remote communication procedures, etc.)?
- ✓ Is there a trial period, say for three months, during which to see how working from home goes and then after that time (or sooner if there are indications of communication issues, technical snags, or client comments) to evaluate what works well and what can be improved?
- ✓ What are the company's short- and long-term goals for employees working remotely and how can you be part of it or help with it?

Take the time to keep in touch with co-workers with these

suggestions...
- Reach out when you have a question
- Get together with and get to know other remote co-workers after work by meeting informally outside office hours
- Congratulate colleagues on milestones such as promotions, awards, birthday, anniversary, and graduations
- Stay connected by using one of the many platforms available like Zoom, RingCentral, and others

Technology

Since technology is part of and integral to the success of working from home, this chapter will cover broadly some of the issues related to technology to pay attention to and stay on top of.

Up-to-date Software, Programs, and Technology
Keep your technology up to date! Make sure the security and anti-virus programs on your computer and other tech devices are working properly with the latest versions installed and running. Back up the work on your computer onto an external hard drive and on cloud on a regular, even weekly, basis. By saving and backing up your documents on cloud, it gives you the option of accessing your documents on any device. You never know when your computer will crash or do an update where it will not let you recover your work. Then you will be happy that you can easily transfer your documents and files from the hard drive onto a new computer. If your (relatively) new-ish computer is running slow, take one of the following steps:

- Organize and clean up the programs and items to free up space (you may have to hire a computer consultant to do this once a year or more often)

- Invest in buying a newer, faster-running computer that has more space and the latest software installed on it
- Call in a computer specialist who can improve or accelerate the speed of your computer (ask family, friends, neighbors, and colleagues for referrals on who they have hired or used as their trusted computer specialist)

A good rule of thumb is that you should be saving money in a savings account each month for larger purchases down the road such as a new computer or laptop, camera, printer, and telephone. Having the best in technology and keeping it properly maintained will be very beneficial in being more efficient with your work time and quick in getting work tasks done. Rather than waiting for a document to load or open for five or ten minutes, you can already be working on that task. Having the best in technology means that you can be confident in being able to finish work tasks in time for deadlines.

> "Having the best in technology and keeping it properly maintained will be very beneficial in being more efficient with your work time and quick in getting work tasks done."

You may also want to keep a record of when you last had your computer maintained and when you renewed or updated your internet security. This will help you know when these things need to be checked and done again. Choose a way and a place — in a document on your computer, handwritten in a notebook, a list by your calendar, a computer appointment pop-up — that works for you and reminds you of these tasks. Maintaining your technology is a key factor in accomplishing your work-from-home goals.

> "Maintaining your technology is a key factor in accomplishing your work-from-home goals."

The Basic Technological Requirements and Equipment

The following is a pretty standard list of technological equipment to have in order to be able to complete all of your work tasks which is given here so that you have the information at hand:

- Laptop(s) and/or desktop computer
- Computer programs (MS Word, PowerPoint, Excel, Photoshop/Adobe Elements, etc.)
- Headset (to minimize background noise while on a video conference or Zoom or Skype call)
- Printer/Scanner
- Phone (or a business number or line, if applicable – consider a phone with more than one line) with voice-mail capability
- Camera (for taking product photos and posting on a website or e-mailing to customers, etc.)

The technological requirements for work-from-home positions are mostly standard from job to job and covered with the above equipment. However, some positions or type of work may require the use of a specific software or program. Make sure to ask about this early on so that you have everything you need for day one on the job. Make it a priority to keep your technology in top-notch condition to stay on top of your work game and bring your best work to the table in the workplace.

Technological Training

Because technology and programs are changing and being updated at such a fast pace, it is important to keep your skills and knowledge relevant to the jobs you want to work at or the industry you work in. If there is a class or program which teaches the skills that you need to know, sign up for and take the course at your earliest opportunity, even if your employer or professional organization will not pay for it. It is up to you as the professional — and it shows that you are a professional — to take courses and training on an as-needed basis (rather than being told by someone from the outside such as an employer or professional organization) to maintain your skills, knowledge, and qualifications in order to do your best work.

Be Careful What You Post

Many articles and books have already been written on this topic and have given this advice but it bears repeating: be careful what you post online. Before venting your frustration/anger/annoyance/complaint about a person, place or something that happened, turn off your phone and computer and calm down. Do not post anything for the rest of the day (or even the next day, if you still feel very upset). Rather, start by figuring out what is bothering you and what can be done to find a solution to the issue or problem to resolve it so that it will not happen again. Or use journaling to clarify your thoughts and cool your reaction to the event. That is a far better response than posting something online which you would regret later and could possibly affect whether you get the job — or not — you want in the future. Remember, things posted online have a way of staying around and resurfacing at the most inconvenient time.

Sign Out and Sign Off

Once you finish work for the day, instead of "relaxing" by surfing the internet looking for videos to watch, messaging friends, or something else, simply sign out and sign off. Spend quality, uninterrupted time with family and friends; read a book; enjoy a leisurely coffee or tea and muffin, cookie, or bagel at a favorite coffee shop; work on a puzzle or play a board game with others; go to the gym; go outside for a walk or a hike, to play tennis, basketball, or soccer; relax by drawing or painting with watercolour or other media; write a letter, story, or article; do a stretch or go dancing; or use holistic services like massage or accupuncture.

The whole point here is to encourage you to take a well-deserved break from staring at a screen and being logged onto technology. You already spend enough time on the computer so get out there, have fun, take your mind off your work, and make some memories!

Takeaway Tips

Staying on top of technology will help you do your best work and complete projects on time. Some things to keep in mind when it comes to technology include...

- ✓ Having up-to-date software, programs, and technology
- ✓ Having basic technological equipment (laptop/computer, phone, printer/copier, camera, etc.)
- ✓ Taking any training on technology as needed
- ✓ Being mindful and careful of what you post online
- ✓ Signing out and signing off when work is done

Working from Home for Life: Suggestions for Different Ages and Stages

The younger generations, Millennials and Generation Z, seem to be especially money-crunched, what with rising food, housing, and education costs, lower wages, less job stability, fewer jobs and more competition for those fewer jobs, along with higher student loans and mortgages. With all of these — and more — financial pressures and struggles, some adults and young adults may question whether they should delay starting a family until they have some basic financial stability. So, what is the reality and the solution to this situation or problem? Is there a way to make your finances work so that starting a family fits into your life plan?

The important thing is not to get discouraged and to go ahead with working toward laying as strong a financial, social, emotional, spiritual, and physical foundation as possible to be ready to start a family and have children. If you are thinking that you will first pay off all your student loans, buy a place of your own, and pay off the mortgage, those are good intentions and goals, but if all that takes ten years — or more — to accomplish, will you realistically still be able to have children

as planned? This concern is particularly important to be considered by women with regard to fertility issues related to increasing age.

This raises the question, whether there are other ways to
work around this issue so that you have a strong base and can
start a family when the time is right for you. Happily, the answer
is yes, there are ideas and solutions that may fit in very well
with your goals and plans for life.

Housing 101

When considering housing options that are affordable, being
creative in this area could be essential. Perhaps looking into a
tiny home or small
home that would
be the right size for
a growing family
with two young
children would be

> "When considering housing options
> that are affordable, being creative
> in this area could be essential."

perfect for keeping housing costs on budget and affordable.
Or, maybe learning more about and visiting a few co-housing
communities is something that would be better aligned with
your housing and community goals. Co-housing provides a
communal space where you can live and work in your own
space but also enjoy interaction with others across different
generations. In co-housing communities, people take turns
making meals together, participating in activities such as
music nights, planting a community garden, learning a new
skill, etc., and working on projects to maintain the property
for the enjoyment of all. Another budget-friendly option is a
pocket neighbourhood with cottages placed around a court-
yard, for example those designed by architect Ross Chapin. Or
look for carriage house apartments (apartments built on top
of a garage) or secondary suites with own entrance. Tiny
home, co-housing, pocket neighbourhood, carriage house

apartment, and secondary suite living are highly conducive as environments that allow and encourage working from home. All that is left is to decide where you are going to call home.

Another solution is to live at home or with family — such as siblings, aunts, uncles, cousins — for as long as you can make that work. This may bring about some eye rolls or other facial expressions and grunts. But this is truly one of the best ways to save up as much money as possible. You can also learn to budget your money properly by creating a financial agreement and paying an agreed-upon rent to your parents/family, paying a portion of utilities and/or groceries, paying for gas and car maintenance, paying for insurance, etc.

Unfortunately, the media has portrayed this positive and practical solution of living at home as somehow being "negative" or a "bad thing" and those who move back home as "boomerang kids". When looking at the big picture, in addition to saving money, there are so many other great benefits to living at home. If you and your family can make it work, some of those perks include:

- More social interaction with people of varying ages which is good for mental and emotional health
- Eating some meals in a communal environment which helps to ensure good eating habits and overall physical and mental health
- Maintaining strong family and community relationships and getting to know family members on a deeper level, which is a bonus not only now but in the long run

When thinking about living at home with parents or other family members — whether as a single adult, couple, or family with young children — it is important to take into account each party's private and personal space as well as noise level considerations. With this in mind, consider different options and ways to create those separate living spaces which will work for all family members:

- Creating a safe secondary or basement suite
- Buying a home with an attic or adding an attic (or room above the garage) to your home
- Converting and/or renovating a garden shed into a safe, livable suite
- Buying a home which already has a carriage house or adding a carriage house to your existing property
- If space and zoning allow, parking a tiny home on wheels on your family's property
- Purchase a home with another family member of your generation, such as a sibling or cousin, to not only bring down housing costs but also own a property. Later, you and the other family member may decide to rent it, thus turning the home into an income property. Make sure, though, to have agreements and contracts reviewed and prepared by a lawyer so that all parties involved know what to expect.

As you can see from the list above, there are several ideas to take into consideration. Keep in mind that each one comes with its own challenges and benefits, work and renovation, regulations, and financial price tag. Whichever you decide to go with, do your research and be patient and understanding along the way.

Working During a Move

Moving is an event which requires time, planning, and energy for packing, storing, and then settling in. To make the event of moving go more smoothly while continuing to work from home, here are some suggestions to help you prepare as much as possible in advance.

Internet Connection

Working remotely means it is important to have at least some access to internet even during a move. Whether that means staying in a hotel, with family or friends, working from a library or café, or arranging some other accommodation, ensure that your plan includes internet connection.

Organization is Key

Throughout the process of packing and moving, stay as organized as you can. This will take some thought and planning. Some tips include marking boxes to know what is in them (be careful, though, with how you label boxes which contain items of value or personal documents), booking moving vans and having enough supplies on hand (tape, boxes, wrapping paper, etc.), and having a calendar to stay on top of dates and appointments.

Books, Notes, and Supplies

As you begin to pack items away ahead of your move, take the time to set aside the books, notes, and office supplies you will require. Having the items needed on hand means that you can focus on work rather than being distracted — and stressed — by looking for the things you need to accomplish work tasks. Mark the moving boxes with content descriptions of office supplies and/or highlight work-related boxes in a notebook with box numbers and box content description to easily find what you need.

Prepare for the Unexpected

What if your lease falls through? What if your move is moved up or delayed due to weather or for another reason? Do you have a backup plan for storage in case you need to store your items someplace temporarily? Do you have an alternate temporary place to stay? Staying in a hotel while looking for another rental adds up quickly and gets expensive.

These are all good questions to ask yourself — and answer — before you move. Having a backup plan and being prepared for the unexpected will leave you ready for any curveball which may come your way during moving time.

Kids

If you are a parent who works from home, you may like to have your child(ren) help you with some tasks. This way, your kids can see and learn about the work you do. They can also observe how you carry out and complete tasks as well as learn from you how to do some of the tasks and thereby gain skills and confidence.

Below are some ideas for how children can lend a hand with your work:
- Sorting receipts according to date
- Looking up phone numbers to call
- Taking photos of products and inventory
- Filling, sealing and addressing envelopes for mailouts
- Helping you practice a sales pitch by being an audience

You will know your children best and can determine which work assignments they are able to handle. As your children learn about and increase confidence in business skills, they may be encouraged to be entrepreneurial and start their own business.

Growing and Raising Your Own Food

Try growing some, or most, of your own food. Start with what you can plant and go from there. If you can grow vegetables such as tomatoes, lettuce, peas, and beans, then grow those. If you can grow fruits instead — raspberries, apples, sour cherries, strawberries — then grow those but keep in mind that fruit trees take more time to bear fruit than bushes. If you can grow a little bit of both fruits and vegetables, then go with that. As you produce some of your own food, take into consideration how you will preserve it — such as canning, dehydrating, or freezing — to enjoy during the winter season. If you have never grown any vegetables or fruits but are open to learning, then begin with reading books and looking at online resources to learn more. If growing your own food is not feasible, then perhaps joining a farm's Community Supported Agriculture program or buying items in bulk is a potential solution. In buying items in bulk, you will want to give some thought to ways you can store the food so that it will last for longer stretches of time.

Do not be afraid to be creative. There are many resources available with information on small-space gardening, container gardening, vertical gardening, community gardening, raised-bed gardening, and much more.

> "Do not be afraid to be creative. There are many resources available with information on gardening."

Of course, how much food you grow will depend on how much space you have, how much garden space you can access to rent, and how much time you have or are willing to devote to it. Can you join and have access to a plot in a community garden? Could you plant a vegetable garden in the corner of a friend or family member's yard, and give them some of the produce that you would grow? Is there another community organization you can partner with to have access to a space for growing food?

Be aware that growing and raising your own food does take time and care in planning, planting, watering, weeding, and harvesting. Before going away on vacation when the weather is warm, arrange for someone to look after your plants by watering, weeding, or harvesting. Reach out to others for help along the way as you find a solution to begin, or expand, a garden area of your own.

If you have an interest in raising chickens for eggs or keeping honeybees to have honey, make sure to check about bylaws regarding keeping poultry and bees for your area. Also make sure to take the time to talk with your neighbors to explain and inform them of your plans. Show your neighbors where you are planning to keep the animals, how you will mitigate any noise or odor, and how you will keep everything safe and clean.

Post-Secondary Options

If you are planning to attend or go back to post-secondary, see if there are things you can do to finish without any debt. Can you take classes online so that you can continue to work? How many scholarships can you apply for and receive? Are there organizations that you, or a family member, belong to which provide scholarships? Can you make passive income? Anything and everything you can do to graduate with no debt, give it a go. Having no debt upon completing school will enable you to start the next chapter of your life on a much more solid financial base.

Build Your Social Network

An important step to take is to build, establish, and maintain your social support network. And here is a secret that the older generations may be keeping to themselves: why do they go to church (besides spiritual and religious reasons)? Because for five, six or even more decades, they have found and maintained a strong social network of friends. Then again, unfortunately, churches have not put in the time or energy in helping organize events and groups which would create social networking for single young adults that the young adults would look forward to and want to take part in every week. Now, it is up to Millennials and Generation Z to prove the older generations wrong and show them that young people can get off the screens, talk to others face-to-face, and have strong friendships.

When you are finished working from home for the day, turn off your screen(s) and either call a friend to talk over the phone or arrange a walk with a neighbour or another 'remoter' on a nice day (even during the winter), go for ice cream, or find an interesting place to explore together or a new event to attend such as a new gallery opening, a new museum exhibit, or a dress rehearsal for a new theatre play. Send birthday cards (and not just Facebook greetings or messages) and thank you notes to friends and family, go skiing for the day, or skating for the afternoon.

Establishing and strengthening your friendships now will be good for the future and when you have children. Thinking ahead, when you have a group of five or six parents who either work from home or have a flexible schedule, why not take turns to look after each other's children one day each week? This will allow both moms and dads to keep up with their jobs and careers (including saving for retirement, kids' college tuitions, etc.), the children will get to observe and learn from adults who each do different work, and the parents will know who is looking after their children during the day. It is a win-win for everyone and avoids everyday reliance on private or government-funded daycare.

Work Date

At a session titled *Working with Virtual Teams* which I was co-presenting at the Editors Canada conference in May 2018 in Saskatoon, SK, one of the attendees shared what I thought was a really great idea: a work date. As many couples are busy with work at all hours of the day, it can make it hard to spend time with your significant other. This is where the work date comes in.

With your significant other, choose a morning, afternoon or evening when you can both work together on work in the same room. It can give both of you the opportunity to learn more about the work each of you does, what their approach and process to work is, and share feedback and ideas on an area you may need a helpful outside viewpoint on. Giving a work date a try can provide something to look forward to in your workweek and can keep communication lines open with your partner on the topic of work.

Because working from home in itself requires a certain degree of creativity and flexibility, it is important to also think a little outside of the box when it comes to meaningful ways to connect, spend time with, and strengthen your relationships with your partner, family members, and friends. Challenge yourself in a fun way to see what other ideas you can come up with.

Finding the Right Work

Finally, finding and landing the work from home job that is the right fit for you — the right hours, wage, type of work, manager, co-workers — can take longer than you think, just like starting and growing your work from home business will take time, too. There are a variety of factors that will determine how soon your business makes the profit you need in order to meet your financial obligations and have a little more left over.

These factors are the current economic picture, taxes and regulations, competition from other similar businesses either online or brick-and-mortar stores, potential versus actual client or customer numbers, and support from family and friends. When faced with the possibility of having less income coming in, a resource to turn to is *How to Survive Without a Salary: Learning how to live the conserver lifestyle* by Charles Long. In this book, the author suggests several practical ways to make it through lean times.

Whatever factors that are beyond your control and affect how soon you can find work from home or make your business a success, the best thing to do is not to get too discouraged but to keep on persevering and doing your best. Even if it takes one, two, or three years to get a solid footing in working from home, now is the time to set the foundation to have a flexible schedule and the work-life balance that complements your lifestyle and goals. Yes, things might get in the way or may cause delay in reaching your goals of working from home and building a foundation on which to buy a home, be debt-free, and start a family. At times, the going may even be downright slow or seem way too challenging. Keep on forging ahead to reach your dreams and you will arrive at where you want to be!

Takeaway Tips

Working from home is possible throughout the various ages and stages of life. Here are some ideas to keep in mind to make it work...

- ✓ Look at available creative, affordable housing options including living at home, adding a safe secondary suite, living in a tiny home or carriage house apartment, being part of a cohousing community, or living in a pocket neighbourhood
- ✓ Grow your own food
- ✓ Consider various post-secondary opportunities including taking classes online
- ✓ Build your social network
- ✓ Set a work date with your partner
- ✓ Find the work that is right for your schedule, skills, and responsibilities

Healthy Home, Healthy You

Looking after your home and health — physically, mentally, and emotionally — is vital to your well-being and bringing your best to work and life. *Healthy Home, Healthy You* provides ways to have a healthy home, stay healthy yourself, and look after you.

In this chapter on maintaining a healthy home, you will learn about using air diffusers to keep the air fresh, opening windows to air out rooms, and cleaning, dusting, and vacuuming on a regular basis. To stay healthy, you will be introduced to using a mini rebounder for exercise, creating a sleep sanctuary in your bedroom for restful sleep, and incorporating essential oils for relaxation.

You will be working from the comfort of your home and will not have to commute to and from work. Still, you will experience stresses related to your work, home, family, finances, and other concerns. There will be deadlines to stick to, colleagues to communicate with over projects and budgets, and clients and customers wanting answers to questions and other information. If that does not make you tired or exhausted yet, there is more. There could be longer hours or overtime hours, paperwork to stay on top of and submit, sales goals and numbers to meet and exceed, and more.

In fact, take a break right now and learn about these ideas for keeping your home healthy and stepping away from work. By taking a breather, you will come back to the task at hand refreshed and recharged.

Healthy Home

Use Chemical-Free Cleaning Products

There is almost nothing that baking soda, vinegar, and tea tree oil cannot clean. When it comes to cleaning your home and doing laundry, make sure to use these natural — and naturally powerful — cleaning products.

Many studies and lots of research shows that the chemicals found in conventional cleaning items are hazardous to one's health in both the short run and long term. Health problems which may result in part from using harmful chemicals include lung and breathing difficulties, cancer, hormone imbalances, and more.

> "When it comes to cleaning your home and doing laundry, make sure to use natural — and naturally powerful — cleaning products."

Another excellent reason to use natural cleaning items is that it is better for the environment — water, plants, air, and animals. By doing your part in choosing to use environmentally-friendly cleaning products, you are helping to create a clean and fresh world not just for you but for future generations as well.

To add a lovely scent to cleaning — whether it is clothes, dishes, or anything else — use a few drops of lavender, peppermint, or citrus essential oils. Lavender is great for relaxation, peppermint is perfect for energy, and orange or lemon are the ones for a cheerful mood.

Air Diffusers and Himalayan Salt Lamps

An air diffuser is a lovely way to give your home a fresh and natural scent. First, put distilled water in an air diffuser and then add about three drops each of one to three essential oils. You can choose to use just one essential oil, such as lavender, or you can create a blend by combining, for example, ylang ylang, frankincense, and myrrh. If you need a scent to help you feel more relaxed or to give you a natural boost of energy, go with peppermint, orange, or experiment with other combinations that work for you. Himalayan salt lamps provide a nice, soft, comforting light and clean the air by attracting airborne pollutants to the salt crystal surface.

Let the Fresh Air In

There is nothing like throwing the windows open and letting the fresh air in! Airing out the rooms in your home gets the stale air out which should result in better quality air that you breathe. Having windows located across from each other is a huge help in getting a nice cross draft to really air out your home and refreshing you with fresh air.

If you live in an area that has a higher level of pollution, whether from traffic, industrial places, construction, or some other source then it would be best to invest in an indoor air cleaner like AirDoctor. Cleaning and ridding indoor air of pollutants, whether by opening the windows or using an air cleaner, helps create more oxygen to reach your lungs to breathe in.

Cleaning, Dusting, and Vacuuming

Regularly cleaning your home and office space — using chemical-free cleaning products — will help keep your home healthy and happy! Dust and wipe counters, desks, and other surfaces; vacuum, sweep, or mop the carpets and floors; and clean anything that needs cleaning including your computer screen and keyboard. You may decide to set aside one morning a week for thoroughly cleaning your home or you may prefer to clean a little bit each day. Whether daily or weekly, choose the cleaning system that will work best for your schedule and what and how much you need to tidy.

Get the family involved in tidying. Family members may learn some practical cleaning tips and tricks along the way plus it will make the time go by quicker and be more fun. It will also help family members realize how much work goes into cleaning a home. When they participate in keeping the home clean and organized, they will value and appreciate a clean and tidy home and the value of the effort to maintain it.

Natural Fibers

Use fibers that are natural such as cotton, wool, bamboo, and silk. Organically grown or untreated fibers are even better. The fabrics which you buy are ones that you will be wearing on your skin and which will be in your home as part of your furniture and drapery, towels, clothes, and linens. Make sure that the air you are breathing is as free as possible from chemicals and Volatile Organic Compounds (VOCs) — found in fabrics and carpets — because you will be spending more time in this environment working from home than ever before.

Maintenance & Projects

Do regular maintenance on your home. This includes things such as checking smoke alarms and carbon monoxide monitors, furnace filter and duct cleaning, roof and shingle replacement/repair, and other house maintenance chores. Keeping a list of things which

"Keeping a list of things which need regular checking and maintaining along with recording when various tasks were done and need to be done will be an immense help."

need regular checking and maintaining along with recording when various tasks were done and need to be done and how long they take to do will be an immense help. For a maintenance checklist, do an online search and pick one that helps you stay on track.

In addition to maintenance, there can also be larger renovation projects. Think of projects that could improve your home in some way and increase your enjoyment of spending time in your house. Examples include:

- Installing solar panels
- Installing in-floor heating
- Adding a window to a room to bring in more natural light
- Replacing a single door with French doors to create the illusion of additional space
- Replacing a sink faucet or shower head with another that permits more adjustability

When embarking on a renovation project, take into account which products will be used and try to select items which do not outgas and with minimal or no use of VOCs found in paints and glues.

Organizing

A healthy home is one that is organized. As mentioned in *The Inspiring Home Office* chapter, begin with what you already have. If you have drawers or cupboards or shelves that are going unused, give those a cleaning and start putting them to use. Drawers, cupboards, and shelves can be used to store clothes, books, games, binders, movies, office supplies, and other useful items available at one's fingertips.

There are many resources available to assist in and provide inspiration for organizing solutions. The key is to create and maintain an organization system which works for you so that items are easily accessible, can be found quickly, and have a place to be stored in to provide a well-organized space free of clutter.

Healthy You
Healthy, Bright Eyes

As working remotely requires a fair amount of time in front of a computer screen, it is vital to look after your eyes and keep them healthy. You want to maintain strong eyesight and have bright eyes that shine. Here are several suggestions to show your eyes some care and love:

- Have a regular eye exam to know what is going on and where things are at with your eyes
- Support the health of your eyes with the vitamins and nutrients they need by eating foods such as fresh, raw carrots, kale, spinach, and taking vitamins A and C
- Help your eyes remain strong and vibrant by drinking Eyebright tea and an adequate amount of water
- Do eye exercises to improve eyesight naturally and consider giving Pinhole Glasses a try
- Minimize stress by decreasing and removing stressors from your life, meditate, and relax your face and eye muscles
- Exercise and give Face Yoga a try
- Do not strain or squint your eyes, and wear sunglasses when it is bright and sunny outside, even in the winter
- Ensure you have enough proper lighting and the correct brightness

Take a Break

Take a few steps away from your desk and take a break. It is as easy as that (or maybe easier said than done!). Go and get a glass of water, a cup of tea or coffee, veggies and dip, or snack on a piece of fruit such as an apple or pear. Remember, if you were working in an office, you would have to get up to go and talk to a colleague at their desk and you would have scheduled break times. So, at your home office, simply take a break. If you need to set a timer to remind yourself to regularly take a break, then do so.

Go for a Walk

Step away from your work and go for a walk around the block or a nearby park or green space. Get some fresh air and start moving to clear your head. Do a few stretches and try some bends to reach your feet to get the blood flowing to your brain, and help you to refocus on work and come up with creative ideas and solutions to any issues that come up.

Garden

Go outside into your yard or on your balcony and do some gardening work, either for a quick 15-minute break during work hours or once work is finished for the day, maybe for a longer period. You can water plants, do some weeding, or start planting the veggie bed for the season. Gardening can be a tool for both relieving built-up stress and frustration and working to calm down. It is also good for creating a form of beauty in the world — and burning calories, too. For those who live in colder, northern climates, use the fall and winter months to clean, prep, and maybe even plant the garden for next year in cold frames or when it gets very cold and snowy, write down the goals and plans for next year's garden. If you live in an apartment with little to no green space, try volunteering at a local community garden or grow as much as you can in pots outside on your balcony.

Get a Massage

Set aside a few hours, at whichever time of the day you prefer, and treat yourself to a well-deserved massage of your choice such as hot stone, aromatherapy, deep tissue, or relaxation massage. Or give an Indian head massage a try for a change. As soon as you start your drive or walk to the spa, take deep breaths, unwind, and start relaxing. This is your time to let the stress melt away, release tension, and let the knots come out.

Allow the calming music in the background float around you. Finish the relaxing time with a cup of tea and going for a leisurely stroll in a park (if the weather is nice and warm) or curl up by the fireplace and watch an uplifting movie or read a book.

Read a Book or Magazine

Take time to read a book you have just borrowed from the library or bought from the bookstore (like this book!). Or maybe you have just received the latest issue of your favorite magazine in the mail. Even if you read for a shorter time, like 10 or 15 minutes, it is still a good break to take from work. It gives your mind a chance to relax, travel to and explore a new world, and think about something else for a while. Having a book or magazine waiting to be read encourages you to take a short, scheduled break during work hours.

Another idea is to read at night, relaxing in an armchair or making yourself comfortable in bed. It will help in slowing and calming down, getting a deeper night's sleep, and being more rested and better prepared emotionally, mentally, and physically for work the next day. Just choose a calming book rather than an exciting thriller.

Stretch

Our bodies are designed to move — they get tight very easily from standing or sitting too long and from being anxious and worried about deadlines, projects, meetings, and other responsibilities. It is important to release tension and stress, and create space in our bodies so that muscles, ligaments, bones, and joints can all move properly and easily.

If you stand or sit at your work space for 30 minutes, take a quick 5-minute break to stretch your legs, back, and arms. Make it a rule that for every 30 minutes of sitting or standing, you will take 5 minutes to move and stretch. Write it on post-it notes if you have to and stick them all over your desk and computer or put a 30-minute timer on your phone to remind you to get up and get stretching.

Rebound

Buy a rebounder and start jumping on the trampoline. Using a rebounder on a regular basis helps to circulate blood and oxygen throughout your body and move toxins out. If you are new to rebounding, start by jumping for two to three minutes at a time. As you are ready, increase the length of time you jump for, perhaps even working up to rebounding twice a day for 15 minutes each time.

Search for different rebounder workouts to keep your rebounding time fun! Rebounding can be a fun way to get some activity in that is gentle on the joints.

Write

You can choose a fancy journal with an inspirational quote or images, a notebook, or just get a few sheets of loose-leaf pages and start writing. Writing can be very relaxing but also very productive — you can get things out of your mind and onto the paper, resulting in less stress for putting pressure on yourself to remember things as you get them written down. Writing does not need to be about writing down your deepest, darkest secrets in a diary. It can be and is so much more than that. It is future-oriented in writing down your goals and tracking your progress in reaching them; it is living in the present when writing a birthday card or a letter to a friend and mailing it; it is having the courage to write that story, poem, or article, and sharing it with readers.

> "Whatever form your writing takes, let it be a place and space where you can go to for healing and quiet reflection, for dreams and future plans — a true break from work and a brief reorientation of your thoughts."

Whatever form your writing takes, whether it is five minutes or two hours a day, let it be a place and space where you can go to for healing and quiet reflection, for dreams and future plans — a true break from work and a brief reorientation of your thoughts.

Journal

Writing in a journal on a regular basis — every morning or evening — is an excellent way to destress and get your thoughts down onto paper. There are many benefits to journaling:

- Decreasing stress and anxiety
- Collecting thoughts and practicing fine motor skills
- Writing down goals and noting progress made in achieving them

There are also several types of journals you can keep:

Career/Work Journal: To change careers or find a new or better job, keep a career/work journal. In this journal, you can note things you notice about yourself such as the time of day you work best, the tasks you enjoy doing, whether you prefer working outside, in a home office, or commuting to an office job, and more as you search for, create, and find your ideal remote work or other job position.

Health/Weight Loss Journal: Record your health goals and the steps you are taking each day to achieve them. This can include things such as the foods you eat and when, the quality of your sleep, exercise, and any events in your life which may affect your health like stressful situations (divorce, job loss, conflicts with co-workers, managers, clients or customers, death in the family, unsupportive family members, etc.) or moments to celebrate (new relationship, being debt-free, graduation, etc.).

Money/Finance Journal: Write down your financial goals and track what you do with the money you have, how you spend, save and invest it, and the progress you make to your financial goals.

Dream Journal: This is best done first thing after waking up. Notice what you dream about and if there are any patterns in your dreams. If you do notice some patterns, you can look into and learn why that might be or what is triggering those images and dreams.

Life Journal: A life journal can be your space to write and remember significant and special moments, days, and events in your life.

Goals Journal: Simply note the goals which you have for various areas of your life — health, money, gardening, travel — and write the things you are doing to reach those goals. For example, if you want to travel somewhere, write down when you want to achieve that, how much you have to save for it, and when you are going to begin booking accommodation — saving information about a romantic inn or a training program presented in a lovely location that would support your plans.

Creativity Journal: Explore different ideas, projects, and ways to express and share your creativity. This might mean making a list of creative things you want to try like sculpture, photography, an art class, a new recipe, or even ideas of a better layout for your home office.

Gratitude Journal: Make it a habit to be thankful for what you have and the good things you are blessed with by starting and keeping a gratitude journal. Every morning and/or evening you can make a list of what you are thankful for. It can get your day started off on a positive note or be a perfect winddown at the end of your day.

Select a journal, diary, or notebook that you like and begin to journal and get to know yourself better.

Visit with Family and Friends

If you have family and friends close by who you get along and enjoy spending time with, make it a point to visit and catch up. Get together to go camping, go on picnics, for reunions, and celebrate weddings and baby showers. It is important to stay socially connected, especially to counteract the potential loneliness of working solo from home and working in front of a screen. Yes, you can connect and talk with family, friends, and co-workers through Facebook, e-mail, phone, and Skype, but meeting friends, family and other people in-person is what creates and builds those networks of support and encouragement during both the good and bad times that life inevitably throws our way.

Give Back

There are many ways to make a helpful difference in your community or to give to a cause that is important to you. It is rewarding to give back and see how you can help have a positive impact.

You can give of your time, on a weekly, monthly, or special event basis, to an organization which has meaning to you. By sharing your time, not only will you be lending a helping hand to the organization with various tasks but you may learn new skills, get to meet new people or get to know some of them better, and perhaps share knowledge that you have gained over the years.

Donating money to a worthwhile cause can be a great way to help out, too. Knowing that you are assisting an organization to carry out its work and mission can be a great feeling. There are many levels of money you can give so choose what works for your budget and whether you want to give as part of a fundraiser, on a monthly basis, or a one-time gift.

Share your skills. If you have the knowledge of carpentry, why not volunteer to teach carpentry once a week to youth? Or perhaps you know how to knit, raise chickens or bees, or edit writing. Find a way of sharing what you know with others.

You could even share what you know through online volunteer opportunities.

Sweet Dreams

Create a sleep sanctuary of your sleeping space. Make it a place that is inviting, relaxing, and special to you. To make your sleep space a true sanctuary, consider the following changes and improvements:

- Keep technology (phones, alarm clocks, and television) outside of the room or unplug the technology each night so that the transmission of Electromagnetic Frequencies (EMFs) within your space is minimized

- Make your room as dark as possible. Install black-out curtains to keep light at bay. A dark room to sleep in makes for a deeper, more restorative sleep which will leave you feeling more refreshed when you wake up.

- Try going to bed when you naturally feel sleepy. It could mean that an earlier bedtime of 9 or 9:30 p.m. is the time when your body is ready for sleep rather than 10 or 11 p.m. or vice versa. Give it a try for a few nights in a row to go to bed at the same time to see if it leaves you feeling rested and ready to tackle the new day.

A percentage of people are affected by wireless and other electronically transmitted magnetic waves. Some people know that they are affected by this and can feel it in the form of headache- or migraine-like symptoms. Others are affected but don't know as they don't experience any symptoms now; however, in another ten or twenty years they may be diagnosed with brain cancer and other brain-related diseases, which electronic and other waves will have partly contributed to.

What can you do to stay healthy, in the short- and long-term, while you work from home using technology? There are actually several things you can do.

First, keep technology (television, computer, phone, CD player, etc.) out of your bedroom/sleeping area. When you go to sleep or take a nap or take a rest, you want to step away completely and relax from any and all technology. You will rest better, feel more refreshed, and thus be able to think more creatively and come up with new ideas and solutions.

Second, do not put your computer next to the television — or if you must, keep the television turned off while you work on the computer. You can always record your favorite shows and watch them later or you can take a break from work, step away from your computer, and enjoy a glass of water and a meal on your lunch break while you watch a half-hour show. In my experience, after a year or so of having the television on during some of the time while I worked on my computer next to the television, I could feel it behind my right ear as my right side was next to the television.

Another option is to have your internet connection coming directly from a wall jack through a wire which is plugged/connected into your computer. This may seem like a step into the past but it does work wonders. In the first place, when you log off/turn off your computer, you truly are stepping away from your work. It also means that even though everyone around you has their wireless signals criss-crossing every which way, you at least are taking control of minimizing the signals that are traveling through your home. To accompany using a wired internet connection, you may want to try giving up your cell phone (or try lessening it to two cell phones for a four-person family rather than a cell phone for each) or at least keep it in airplane mode when not in use. Going back to a landline is a healthier option, preventing EMF energy to be close to your body, and also a practical one as you now have a home office with an accessible in-wall phone jack.

Takeaway Tips

It is important to create a healthy home environment. Ways to do that are to...

- ✓ Use chemical-free cleaning products
- ✓ Use an air diffuser
- ✓ Let the fresh air in
- ✓ Clean, dust, and vacuum
- ✓ Use natural fibers
- ✓ Do regular maintenance and projects
- ✓ Organize

As you create a healthy environment in your home, make sure to look after you by...

- Looking after your eyes to make sure they are healthy, strong, and bright
- Taking a break
- Writing and/or reading
- Journaling
- Rebounding and exercising
- Visiting with family and friends
- Giving back
- Getting proper sleep

Keeping on Learning

Keeping your skills and knowledge up-to-date is essential to your success in your job and career. Depending on your educational background and current work, you may already belong to a profcssional organization which requires a certain number of courses or hours each year to satisfy professional development requirements.

In your work-from-home job, if you work for a company, then they may send you on and perhaps pay for their employees to take one or two courses a year. If your work includes selling courses or products, you might be asked to attend one of the courses or try the products. By taking the course and trying the product, you will gain lots of knowledge and confidence in what the service or product is about and you will be much better prepared to satisfactorily answer clients' questions.

The other professional development option is for you to take charge of it yourself. That means taking courses, watching videos, and reading magazines and books whenever you need to learn a new skill or find out more about a subject or topic. This aspect of professional development puts the responsibility on you to know when you need to upgrade or add to your skills, and to take the initiative to find the right program which gives the best quality of instruction.

Ways to Keep on Learning

Magazines (MoneySense, Writer's Digest, Professional Artist, The Writer, and other publications in your area of expertise or interest)

Reading through magazines filled with advice on how to submit work, trying new techniques to add oomph to your job, or finding online support groups in your occupation can provide new ideas and inspiration to improve your work and take it to the next level. You will also learn about the leaders and experts in your field.

Continuing Education

Many universities, colleges, and other education providers, such as Centre of Excellence, offer courses and diploma and certificate programs. Post-secondary institutions may offer classes through their Continuing Education department. Most courses are available to be taken in either on-campus or online formats. Post-secondary schools are beginning to realize that they need to offer this choice in formats to stay competitive. Students have different demands on their time so online and on-campus course and program choices go a long way in students taking the step to keep their skills and knowledge relevant.

Find a Mentor

Learn from someone you admire, someone who has found and achieved success in working from home or starting a business. They can share insight, wisdom, and encouragement. Your mentor can tell you what works and what does not, what to try, and what to watch out for. Your mentor can be your professor from college or university, a co-worker or manager from a job you held, a friend, or even a family member.

Podcasts and Recordings

Listening to challenging, inspiring, and motivating speakers on podcasts and recordings can give you new ideas and insight into areas where you may need to grow your skills. Podcasts and recordings can range from inspirational, to get you on the path of reaching your goal of working from home, to personal finances advice to more in-depth talks to gain knowledge for learning about a topic of interest to you.

Workshops, Seminars and Webinars

Taking place on weekends or as evening offerings, workshops and seminars can be great places and opportunities to learn from leaders and experts. They can teach tools and offer tips, suggestions, and techniques on topics such as Time Management Skills, Communicating with Co-Workers, and Organizing Your Work Space which all lead to your success in working from home. Attending workshops and seminars in-person provides a nice break away from the computer screen and home office and gets you out mingling and talking with others and practicing your networking skills.

Books

There are many books to find and read on the various aspects of working from home and other topics related to working, business, career development, etc. Start with this list of books (this list, along with more books, is also included at the end of this book in **Appendix B – Resources**) to expand your knowledge, gain perspective, and learn new skills by putting into practice some of the suggestions:

- *Remote: Office Not Required* by Jason Fried and David Heinemeier Hansson
- *The Laptop Millionaire: How Anyone Can Escape the 9 to 5 and Make Money Online* by Mark Anastasi

- *Multiple Streams of Internet Income: How Ordinary People Make Extraordinary Money Online* by Robert G. Allen
- *There Is Life After College: What Parents and Students Should Know About Navigating School to Prepare for the Jobs of Tomorrow* by Jeffrey J. Selingo
- *The 4-Hour Workweek: Escape 9-5, Live Anywhere, and Join the New Rich (Expanded and Updated)* by Timothy Ferriss
- *The 10% Entrepreneur: Live Your Startup Dream Without Quitting Your Day Job* by Patrick J. McGinnis
- *ECOpreneuring: Putting Purpose and the Planet before Profits* by John Ivanko and Lisa Kivirist
- *Making a Living While Making a Difference: Conscious Careers in an Era of Interdependence* by Melissa Everett
- *Make Yourself at Home: Design Your Space to Discover Your True Self* by Moorea Seal (more specifically, see Chapter 4 on *Home Office*)
- *The Comeback: How Today's Moms Reenter the Workplace Successfully* by Cheryl Casone
- *Work Together Anywhere: A Handbook on Working Remotely Successfully for Individuals, Teams & Managers* by Lisette Sutherland & K. Janene-Nelson
- *Great Pajama Jobs: Your Complete Guide to Working from Home* by Kerry Hannon
- *The Ultimate Guide to Remote Work: How to Grow, Manage, and Work with Remote Teams* by Wade Foster and the Zapier Team
- *Will Work from Home: Earn the Cash — Without the Commute* by Tory Johnson and Robyn Freedman Spizman

There are many options and opportunities readily available to you as you pursue keeping your skills and knowledge up-to-date. Take the time to research the possibilities to decide what would work best for you — whether that is an online course or an in-person workshop — and then go for it.

> "There are many options and opportunities readily available to you as you pursue keeping your skills and knowledge up-to-date."

Above all, make sure to enjoy the process of learning new things. Ask questions, read, discuss, and listen so that you are able to learn as much as you can.

Takeaway Tips

There are many ways to keep your skills and knowledge up-to-date. Consider some of the following professional development resources and options...

- ✓ Magazines – in your area of expertise or on topics of interest to you
- ✓ Continuing education
- ✓ A mentor
- ✓ Podcasts and recordings
- ✓ Workshops, seminars and webinars
- ✓ Books

Part 2

Extraordinary People
Who Work from Home

The Ivanko and Kivirist Family: At Home in Wisconsin, United States

Left to Right: Liam Kivirist, John Ivanko and Lisa Kivirist on their farm in Wisconsin. Photo credit: Megan Monday for Love Wisconsin (lovewi.com).

Interview with John Ivanko and Lisa Kivirist, authors of 'ECOpreneuring: Putting Purpose and the Planet before Profits', 'Soil Sisters: A Toolkit for Women Farmers', 'Homemade for Sale,' 'Farmstead Chef,' 'Rural Renaissance', and 'Edible Earth', and innkeepers of Inn Serendipity Bed & Breakfast.

Q: You are the authors of the book 'ECOpreneuring: Putting Purpose and the Planet before Profits', published in 2008. Tell me in your own words what is ECOpreneuring and in what ways is it complementary to working from home?

ECOpreneuring is about finding your own life passion and then, through the business you create, making the world a better place. Life is too short to be working at a job, perhaps stuck in an office cubicle, working hard to make someone else richer, like a CEO or shareholders.

Rather than work hard for money, we try to make our limited financial resources work hard for us. Since we own our home, why not work from a home office? Instead of hours commuting to work, we just head to our second-floor office for our work on books we author, articles we write for national magazines like Mother Earth News, presentations we prepare and, for John, photography he edits in post-processing. When we're ready for lunch, we prepare it in [the] kitchen, usually with organic vegetables we grow on site and usually with our son, who was home schooled, and has his own home-based enterprises. That saves us thousands each year in purchased foods at restaurants or grocery stores. When we're in the B&B season, our two Inn Serendipity guest rooms, each of which have their own bathroom, are rented out.

In total, about 24-percent of our home is used for business purposes, which means expenses related to these rooms are tax-deductible. Plus, our business pays us rent for the use of our home for the business. From our ecological perspective, the business also invests in renewable energy systems to power the home office and other enterprises operated from our property, which is also a small-scale organic farm. We're incredibly diversified, which we've found provides stability, flexibility and freedom to work on the projects most interesting to us.

To every extent possible, we select work and investments that don't destroy or deplete the planet, but instead, restore, revitalize or renew. For example, we don't just serve the average breakfast at Inn Serendipity Bed & Breakfast, we serve a hearty, vegetarian meal based on what we call a "hundred-foot diet" where nearly all the organically-grown ingredients come from within a hundred feet of our back door; for what we don't grow, the rest is procured locally or from organic suppliers via our regional Willy Street Co-op.

Working from home remains the core and vital component of our lifestyle and livelihood. We cut out many expenses. There's no commute or take-out lunches in Styrofoam containers. More importantly, it's what we gain through a home-based livelihood. We control our schedules and time. We work when it is best for our biorhythms, not someone else's clock. For example, Lisa has always been a crazy early morning bird and works best when she can focus during that 5 am – 9 am time block. Not your typical "office hours," but it works for her!

Q: Is there any specific advice you would give to younger generations, before they start having families or while they are young, for steps to take now to having a flexible schedule while working at something they love?

Figure out what it is that gets you excited, passionate and provides meaning. Then build your life around that. A purpose-driven life is so much more meaningful, rewarding and fulfilling than a job that just juices your bank account, 401(k) or stock options. As we write in ECOpreneuring: Who wants to be the richest person in the cemetery?

The question for us has never been: How much do I need to earn a living? Rather, it's been how do I learn to live well on what I earn through a livelihood that nourishes my soul, magnifies my talents while providing the needed income base. Live below your means. Buy only what you really need and do so with cash, or with a credit card that you pay off every month. If you can, put off getting married or starting a family until your self-employed livelihood has a decorum of stability. Don't let financial stress potentially ruin a beautiful start to a marriage or bringing a child into the world.

From the start, we were serious about being home-based entrepreneurs. What could we eliminate in terms of expenses to make our dream come true? In our case, a lot. One car [a plug-in hybrid Toyota Prius Prime] is shared between us; it's super-fuel efficient, so every business mile we put on it is reimbursed to us at the IRS vehicle rate at a rate more than what the car takes to operate. No cable TV, digital music service or even a smartphone. We get our books, music and movies for free from our local library. By stripping away living expenses and working from a home office, it opens up more creative time to do the things we want to do.

It also helps to develop your entrepreneurial, self-employment savvy, ideally prior to making the full jump or at least to have one person in the partnership with some experience. In our case, John had successfully run several small businesses in college where he had even set up a sub-chapter S corporation, which helped us a lot in realizing the importance of record keeping and organizing one's business. This can be a tricky road for some folks to navigate, especially if you have always been on a payroll. As your own boss of your home business, you can now deduct your miles, office rent and even business meals when meeting with clients.

For us, it [has] always been about the quality of life, the vibrancy of our community and the amazing control and flexibility we have over our day-to-day life, both professionally and personally. Once we left the cubicle at a very young age of 25, we never looked back.

Q: How has ECOpreneuring changed since the publishing of your book in 2008? How do you see ECOpreneuring adapting and changing in the next ten to twenty years?

In many ways, ECOpreneuring has become even more relevant, important and essential in helping restore [the] Earth's failing ecosystems and solving the most pressing issues of our time, even if − or perhaps especially because − the political will and governmental policies are glaringly absent. From climate change and loss of biodiversity to mountains of debt and massive islands of plastic floating in the oceans [which] are growing ever larger, we need business to become the engine for change, making the world and our communities better, healthier and more resilient to the changes we face as a result of many of the issues.

At some point, the pendulum of worldview, social discourse and harsh realities of our perilous future will swing back mightily. Nearly everyone will drive cars that do not have an internal combustion engine, or ride around in autonomous, shared-use electric vehicles. There will be no plastic bags handed out at grocery stores. Communities will become immensely walkable, with people encouraged to work from home offices whenever possible. Lawns will become a food oasis. And ecopreneurs will be guiding and leading these changes, every step of the way.

Q: In your experience consulting and working with businesses and ECOpreneurs, what are some of the skills, traits, and qualities needed to be successful or "make it" as an ecopreneur? Are there ways to develop those skills, traits, and qualities?

We'd argue that we're all ecopreneurs, or will be very soon. With the slow unraveling of our environment, mounting impacts resulting from climate change and rather dubious and fragile financial underpinnings of our current economic system, at the ecopreneurs' core, they are problem solving through their business. Maybe it's making a healthier food product, providing a service missing in your community [by] perhaps making all deliveries on bicycle or foot, or powering their business completely with renewable energy, ecopreneurs seize the opportunity to transform their enterprise into one that follows a triple bottom line: care for people, planet and profit.

Ecopreneurs are different from entrepreneurs in one key

facet, and that's the profit motive. Both tend to solve problems, make changes, reinvent how we do things or live. However, ecopreneurs hold social and ecological considerations above the almighty dollar. It's not how much money you earn that makes your business successful or great. How you earn is more important than what you earn. In many cases, what makes a business successful may be the amount of surplus renewable energy produced by the business, the increase in organic food available locally, or the number of articles that address climate change. Keep in mind, according to the IRS, to be in business, the business only needs to make some profit three of every five years.

In Lisa's work with women farmers and food entrepreneurs and in her book, *Soil Sisters: A Toolkit for Women Farmers*, she particularly focuses on the female side of ecopreneuring. Women can thrive as ecopreneurs when given the opportunity to merge a passion for sustainability with self-employed livelihood. This can readily happen in farm-based businesses as women can creatively diversify and run multiple businesses from home, all of which add up to a healthy livelihood, from farmstays to value-added products under cottage food law which we write about extensively in our Homemade for Sale book.

We'd argue that most of us are hard-wired to care for others and the planet. It's in our nature to love to go for walks on beaches, enjoy sunsets, bite into a juicy peach, and laugh with friends. We want to do the right thing, but doing the thing right can be hard when we're getting conflicting messages from some businesses, government officials, the news media, or neighbors. We need to trust our intuition more and ignore the societal mantras of "bigger is better" or "money equals success." Joy in our work and happiness with our life are far more valuable to us. So we work hard, try to listen mindfully, and model much of what we do as closely as we can to how it works in ecological systems. For example, our homemade cottage food products like sauerkraut, pickles and breads, have no ingredients you can't pronounce!

Q: What are the unique advantages and disadvantages, opportunities and challenges to ECOpreneuring in the United States? Is the environment different in Canada and in what way?

Regardless of the political climate or leadership, the United States remains a nation supportive of entrepreneurs and small business. This is something to understand and use to our advantage. As ecopreneurs, "advantage" also relates to sustainability. For example, the current IRS rate of mileage reimbursement is 53.5 cents per mile. The mileage reimbursement rate is based on the whole fleet of vehicles, including the most inefficient ones like sport utility vehicles, jeeps and luxury cars. We drive a plug-in hybrid Toyota Prius Prime, which we charge on-farm with electricity we generated with our renewable energy systems. At the current reimbursement rate, we can reimburse ourselves at a rate higher than what it costs to operate the vehicle, so it's better for both our bottom line and the environment.

Like any business, an ecopreneurial enterprise needs customers who would like to buy their product or service. We've found that not only are there plenty of customers who want to support your green business without destroying the planet, they're a loyal, passionate and committed bunch. Let them support your efforts to make the world a better place. We find we don't need to be everything to everyone. As in nature with its ecological niches, choose your ecopreneurial niche carefully and by all means, diversify.

New Society Publishers, the publisher for our books *ECOpreneuring*, *Homemade for Sale*, *Soil Sisters*, *Farmstead Chef* and *Rural Renaissance*, is based in Canada. These books are printed on Forest Stewardship Council certified, 100-percent old grown forest-free paper by another company, also in Canada. Canadians have some of the most livable cities in the world and many of its citizens share values related to eating health foods, enjoying the outdoors, and working in a way that does not ruin the planet. So, becoming an ecopreneur in Canada would afford the same opportunities and potentially find eager customers just as likely, if not more so, than in the USA.

Q: How has technology made it easier and/or more challenging to find new customers/clients/companies/ businesses to work with?

Technology seems to be, in many ways, the great equalizer, if used wisely and effectively. On the one hand, computers, social media, and electronic networks have opened up massive new markets for many of our income-generating activities, from freelance writing and authoring books to selling photography and offering on-farm workshops related to starting food product business from your home thanks to the ever-expanding cottage food laws in nearly every state in the US. What used to cost hundreds of dollars a year for the machine to process credit cards can be done, simply, with a free Square device inserted into a smart phone or tablet. Websites can now be designed for free.

On the flip side, however, technology has flooded the market with amazing photography, taken with smartphones, and turned everyone into citizen journalists if they choose to launch their own blog. The result has been a spiraling downward of fees related to creative content generation. Magazines no longer need to pay for photos when they're free or very low cost online. So, for some industries, it's been a boom while others, like newspapers and magazines, a decline.

For the tech savvy, often glued to their smartphone, technology can both sap precious time and transform your marketing into precise targeting that brings customers through your doors with practically no money spent at all. The key is figuring out how to make it work best for you. That said, once you do, it's not over. The thing with technology is that it keeps changing and evolving. Technology demands a continuous investment of time, energy and knowledge acquisition. It's okay if technology is not your thing; for your home-based business, it might not have to be. It's unlikely that we will ever take electronic reservations for our Inn Serendipity. We like to know our potential customers before they book, to make sure our farmstay bed & breakfast experience is what they're looking for. For example, some folks really like their OJ and bacon for breakfast; our place has neither. Orange juice is definitely not local and we specialize in vegetarian and vegan breakfasts. With an online booking system, we'd lose control of the transaction. Our goal with the business is to create memorable experiences for guests, not put heads on beds.

Technology has helped transform our very diversified and multifaceted enterprise into one that's agile, interconnected, and largely self-sustaining. Our business is completely powered by the sun and produces more renewable energy than we use; we get paid by our utility. During the summer growing season, we meet nearly 70-percent of our food needs for ourselves and for organic ingredients at Inn Serendipity Bed & Breakfast. John has gone from DSLR photography into aerial videography and photography with a DJI Phantom 4 Pro+ drone. Also, thanks to Liam, we offer virtual reality demos with Oculus Rift along with the opportunity for B&B guests to play a game of chess outside with our life-size chess set.

Photo of John Ivanko and Lisa Kivirist's farm and Bed & Breakfast,
Inn Serendipity, in Wisconsin shown in a beautiful summer light.
Photo credit: John D. Ivanko Photography
(https://jo5094.wixsite.com/johnivanko).

An aerial view of John Ivanko and Lisa Kivirist's Inn Serendipity farm in
Wisconsin lit by the setting sun in the fall. Photo credit: John D. Ivanko
Photography (https://jo5094.wixsite.com/johnivanko).

Lisa Kivirist shown working in her home office space in Wisconsin. Lisa has a padded mat to stand on, which adds extra support and cushioning, and has lots of natural light coming in through the window. Lisa Kivirist uses a ClassicRiser Standing Desk by FlexiSpot so she can stand or sit as she works. Changing positions frequently, whether at the desk or weeding a row in the growing fields, is one way she cares for her body. Yoga is another. Photo credit: John D. Ivanko Photography (https://jo5094.wixsite.com/johnivanko).

Steve Maxwell: Living and Working on Manitoulin Island in Ontario, Canada

Photo of Steve Maxwell shown in his workshop at home.
Photo credit: Steve Maxwell (www.baileylineroad.com).

Interview with Steve Maxwell, owner and operator of Bailey Line Road on Manitoulin Island. Steve has "...been writing, taking photos, making videos, building furniture, houses and working with stone for more than 30 years" (quote taken from www.baileylineroad.com/steve-maxwell-biography/).

Q: What are the opportunities and challenges encountered in working from home in rural northern Ontario? What adjustments need to be made to accommodate working from home?

The thing I like best about working from home is that geography never enters the equation. Working from home for me on Manitoulin Island is the same as working from home anywhere else. Actually, the term "working from home" isn't really accurate. I can work productively from wherever I can sit with my laptop. This has allowed me much more freedom in life, especially when it comes to my kids. My wife and I have travelled to watch our kids participate in events around the world, we can take trips on short notice, and my work time is entirely flexible. If I want to do something beyond money work during the day, I can make up for it in the evening. The work that supports our family goes with me.

Q: What support is there for working from home in the local community? Does the Ontario government provide any form of support, such as programs or funding?

There's no particular government support for people working from home where I live, and this is just as it should be. If work can't fund itself without relying on money taken from the pockets of other people by government, then that work is not worth doing. I do appreciate the government involvement in getting high-speed internet to my area in 2016, but beyond that I'm good as-is.

Q: How can both Ontario and Canada improve in their support of Canadians working from home? Or is that an area that private companies need to progress in rather than have government regulation?

It's up to the individual home worker to make the economics happen. Government has a long track record of being bad at business. The best thing government can do is get out of the way of businesses large and small. Canadian governments, in particular, put a terrible burden on some business sectors. Not so much mine, but many small businesses are smothering to death under unbelievable and pointless government rules that have creeped in over the last 20 years. Truly good government recognizes that it should be involved as little as possible in the economy.

Q: How does being a team as a couple or having the whole family involved in the business from home play a role in making working from home a success or not? What would be your main piece of advice to those in the same situation who may be thinking of working from home?

Working from home has been a fabulous thing for our kids. Growing up with two parents at home all the time on our country property has been very beneficial for the children and my wife and me. When I started working from home in 1988, my wife and I shared the job of earning money. In 1998 we decided to specialize. My wife quit her job as a registered nurse and I took on the responsibility of earning all the money for our family. My wife took on the role of taking care of our home full time. It's been a great arrangement. Our family income has risen because I'm free to do my thing, and our home is a clean, orderly place filled with the great smells of home cooking. It's a shame that so many young people these days have never known the beauty that comes from the traditional division of labour in the family. Keeping the home is the most important work in the world. There is no greater career than a homemaker who takes this work seriously. My career and the money I earn is only valuable to the extent that it pays for the things my wife buys to make our home comfortable, enjoyable, clean and fun. She sits at the top of the economy as far as I'm concerned.

All this said, working from home can be heaven or quite the opposite. Success or failure comes down to a few things:

1. You need to be good at self-motivation. Without the personal drive to happily work productively at least 40 hours per week, week after week and year after year without a boss, working from home will never succeed.

2. You need to have a financially valuable skill. Just because you can do something or make something at home, does not mean you can be productive enough to earn suffi-

ciently.

3. Digital work is the best kind of work to do from home. You're at a big disadvantage making most physical things at home because you're competing against big factories around the world. Digital work operates on a much more level playing field.

4. You need to be entrepreneurial to thrive working from home. The world has changed a lot over the last 30 years that I've been working from home, and my work today is much different and more complex than it was in 1988 when I started. It had to change to remain profitable.

The time and money saved by not commuting has allowed me the time needed to build my own house without help. Seeing the example of my own work over the years, my oldest son, Robert, has decided to do the same thing. He lives in a house on our country property that we built together because I had the flexibility in my work day to help him build without a mortgage. He works from home in the digital realm and we often collaborate on projects. Robert has learned to do work that I haven't, so we're both better off for the collaboration we do. He has breakfast, lunch and supper with his wife and their baby daughter, and we all get together for meals and family movie nights once or twice a week. Robert and I work out together in our home weight training gym during the work day. We're both very thankful for the blessings that working from home gives us and our families. It's a great thing for those with the temperament and skills to make it happen.

An aerial view of Steve Maxwell's property on beautiful Manitoulin Island, Ontario. Photo credit: Steve Maxwell (www.baileylineroad.com/).

Photo of Steve Maxwell's home on his property on Manitoulin Island with a nice wrap-around porch and lots of sunlight.
Photo credit: Steve Maxwell. (www.baileylineroad.com/)

*Steve Maxwell's workshop and office space on Manitoulin Island.
Steve has a well-organized office where he has space for his computer so
that he can write articles and take videos, to explain and demonstrate
steps as he works on projects, and has space in his workshop for the tools
he needs to work on projects. Photo credit: Steve Maxwell
(www.baileylineroad.com).*

Carolina Thompson: City-based Dayhome Owner and Operator in Alberta, Canada

Photo of Edmonton-based dayhome owner and operator, Carolina Thompson. Photo credit: Carolina Thompson.

Interview with Carolina Thompson who tells about her love of working with families and children as a dayhome owner and operator, all while being able to work from home. Being a dayhome operator allows her to spend time with her family.

Q: In what ways has your work as a dayhome owner and operator changed in the last year? How have you adjusted and what measures have you taken to keep children and families safe?

I have had a huge reduction in demand for my services this past year, because a lot of people were without work, and didn't need childcare. I lost all my clients during the first wave of Covid, and then they came back after a few weeks, but then I lost them all again in the second wave, and so far, haven't been able to get any back. To adjust to the pandemic, I made sure that things like eating surfaces and door handles etc. were more frequently sanitized. We were unable to go to the park for a while because of restrictions and also, we couldn't take the bus all year because of the dangers of Covid. The criteria for illness were made more strict, so that children with minor symptoms of a cold were unable to come into my care until they had had a negative Covid test result. It has been a difficult year for sure.

Q: What does it feel like to work from home in a field that might not usually be considered as a typical work from home job? Are there some memorable reactions from people when you mention that your job is a work from home one?

People often confuse my job with a daycare. Then I have to clarify that since I take care of children from my own home, I am a dayhome provider, not a daycare worker. That's about the extent of people's confusion though, since running a dayhome is a pretty common occupation here in my city.

Q: What are the advantages and disadvantages to working from home in a larger city, such as Edmonton, in Alberta?

The advantage is that there are many families to draw from as potential clients. The disadvantage is that there is so much competition from other dayhomes in the area.

Q: What support is there for working from home in the local community of Edmonton? Does the Alberta government provide any form of support, such as programs or funding?

The government allowed me to take my Level 1 in childcare

for free, and because I have that certification and am contracted under a registered dayhome agency, the government also pays me an extra $150/month for each child under 18 months old that I care for, and also an extra $2.14 for every hour that I'm working, up to $387.34/month.

Q: How can both Alberta and Canada improve in their support of Canadians working from home? Or is that an area that private companies need to progress in rather than to have government regulation?

I feel that both the government and private companies need to do more to explore the options and see which of their existing jobs could be from the comfort of an employee's home. I feel that there is an obsession with having employees physically at a workplace, because managers don't want to dilute their company culture, but I feel that the sacrifices would be outweighed by benefits to the workers.

Q: How does a well-organized work space increase productivity and efficiency? What are the most important elements that make for a well-organized work space?

I am probably the wrong person to ask this question of, because I am not very organized myself! In my job, I feel that lots of room is important, because the kids need room to run and play. I wish that my house was larger than it is, but it works. It is important to schedule your day with the kids as well, but I find that one has to be very flexible with this schedule, because so often it is necessary to make allowances for nap times or for cranky hungry toddlers.

Q: What are the benefits and drawbacks to working from home part-time and full-time? What are the reactions from people when they learn that you work from home?

To me, the biggest benefit of my job is that I can make

money while still staying at home with my kids. That's HUGE to me, and was the driving motivation behind my choice to run a dayhome in the first place. The downside is that often we're stuck in the house because we don't have a large enough car to transport everyone, so in the winter time we can go a bit stir-crazy. I enjoy working as a dayhome provider part-time more than I do full-time, because I like to get a day or two off in the week to just get out and do some grocery shopping, or take my kids to a fun activity or something. When people hear that I get to work from home with my kids, they are often jealous, and start asking lots of questions about how to become a dayhome provider themselves, which I am always happy to answer.

Carolina Thompson's home office where she completes her administration tasks for the dayhome she owns and operates in Edmonton. Under Carolina's desk are plenty of drawers for storing paper and supplies when not in use. This helps keep her workspace tidy, clean, and free of clutter. Photo credit: Carolina Thompson.

The well-organized front entryway of Carolina Thompson's dayhome. There is a bulletin board where notices are posted and lots of space for coats, scarves, and more. Photo credit: Carolina Thompson.

The bright and spacious playroom (with lots of fun toys!) for children to play in at Carolina Thompson's Edmonton dayhome. Photo credit: Carolina Thompson.

Bob Britton: Sales, Marketing, and Working from Home in Texas, United States

Photo of Bob Britton, owner of
Sales Enablement Sherpas, based in Texas.
Photo credit: Bob Britton (www.sesherpas.com)

Interview with Bob Britton, owner of Sales Enablement Sherpas (www.sesherpas.com), a company based in Texas which helps others all over the world reach their sales goals.

Q: In what ways does knowledge and confidence in sales help someone who is self-employed and working from home?

Obviously, being able to generate revenue is an absolute necessity for anyone who is self-employed and working from home. There are two primary ways to generate revenue — marketing, and sales, which are two different things. If you want to generate revenue through marketing, then you must be savvy with website design, e-commerce, graphics, videos, and messaging, or you can outsource any of these things if you don't yet have the skillsets or time to do it on your own. To get an idea of what revenue generation by marketing is, think of Dell, or Amazon, or any place online where you never interact with another human being; you just choose what you want from a list that's provided to you, pay for it with a credit card or PayPal, and it magically appears on your doorstep within a few days, or even hours! Without human to human interaction, it's not really sales — it's marketing. And, you can make a nice living off that from your home, without ever stepping foot outside, if you have something a lot of people want.

Sales, on the other hand, starts with marketing (you'll need a website, some messaging, probably some video content to grab peoples' attention, and so on), which then extends into interacting with people to discover what they need and want, then meeting those needs and wants with what you can provide. Think of revenue generation by marketing as casting a some-what wide net to see what you can catch, and sales as spear-fishing for a specific type of fish. If you are selling, self-employed, and working from home, then you need to treat your home (or at least part of it) as your office and base of operations, from which you'll go out to meet your prospects and clients, either virtually like we're all doing now with COVID-19 and/or in person when things start to ease up a bit.

My profession is Sales Enablement, which means part of what I do is train people how to sell. I have heard a lot of people say that sales isn't for them. Well, I've got news for you: We're all sellers, whether we realize it or not! We sell things every day. You sell your significant other on going to your restaurant instead of theirs. You sell your friends on where to go out tonight. You sell yourself every time you meet somebody new you want to get to know better! Sales starts with having confidence in yourself and your abilities and knowing that you're never going to know it all, but you'll probably be able to figure it out as you go. Then, what's most important about sales is this: It's not about you or what you have to offer, it's about your customer. It's always about them, not you. If you make sales about yourself and your products or services, then you're doing it wrong and it will be an uphill battle the whole way. Make it about the customer and there's a good probability you'll be more successful than you ever imagined.

Q: How have you adapted to changes you have faced over the years in working from home? Is there a way to prepare for or make the transition easier when the changes come?

Working from home has become easier because the technology once only available to [small businesses] (SMBs) and larger companies is now available to anyone. You used to need an expensive video teleconferencing system to have a virtual face to face conversation and bringing one of those home with you was out of the question. Now, all you need is the camera on your laptop and a decent pair of headphones, and you can get face to face with anyone anywhere in the world, right from your home office! Or, for that matter, you can use your mobile phone as your video teleconferencing system. Geography is no longer an issue. You can step it up a bit like I do with a green screen, a professional mic, and a little studio lighting, but it's not absolutely necessary. Even much of the software you'll need is opensource and free.

The biggest challenge in working from home is being self-disciplined. You must treat it like a regular job. Dress appropriately because you never know who you'll be meeting with on camera at any given time. Set rules and boundaries with others in the house so you're not disturbed during the time you're working. Did I mention the camera...? Yes, these days it's important that you make the effort to not be shy and turn that thing on! Even if the other person you're connecting with on Zoom doesn't turn their camera on, keep yours on and be there with them. Take the initiative. And, if you're self-employed, remember this: Every day, you wake up unemployed and you have to go out and find work. And turn your camera on...

Q: What prepared and decided you to start your own company and work remotely from home?

There's a certain amount of pride, autonomy, and sheer terror in owning your own business. What prepared me was having jobs early on where I was either paid commission (like working the front of the house in a restaurant for tips) and seeking out managerial jobs where you learn the value of teamwork. Next was my military career, where leadership takes on a whole different meaning and you learn more about how you behave under stress than you ever could in most civilian occupations. And, of course, getting my MBA (from Southern New Hampshire University (SNHU)) was huge in helping me understand business dynamics and what it took to put a company together.

Why did I decide to start my own business? Because I believe in what I do and know the value I can bring to my customers. Another reason is the Sword of Damocles always hanging over your head when you're an "at will" employee; one or two bad quarters and many companies will punch that layoff button faster than somebody reaching for their buzzer when playing Jeopardy! I've been laid off a couple of times, and it's like a gut punch, not because I didn't think I'd be able to find another job, but because the reason I got laid off was beyond my direct control. When you have your own business, it's yours. Win or lose, feast or famine, it's all on you. Plus, most people leave a job because of their direct boss, so you'd better like yourself if you want to stay in business!

Bob's desk is spacious, having room for two
computer monitors and a laptop.
Photo credit: Bob Britton (www.sesherpas.com)

The home office for Bob's company, Sales Enablement Sherpas. Bob's desk
is spacious, having room for two computer monitors and a tablet. The
map on the wall adds a personal touch to the space, perhaps a reminder of
places on one's bucket list to travel to.
Photo credit: Bob Britton (www.sesherpas.com)

This photo shows the green screen which Bob has in his home office and uses as a background for virtual calls. Bob's office space also has a bookshelf which is home to books and more.
Photo credit: Bob Britton (www.sesherpas.com)

Natalie and Rolf Falkenberg: Happy Dwellers in Rural Alberta, Canada

Interview with Natalie and Rolf Falkenberg who share about the benefits and challenges of working from home in rural Alberta. This couple talks about what it is like working and living together full-time and what is needed to make that work.

Q: What are the benefits and challenges to working from home together for the same company but in different positions? How do you handle your work spaces – separate in the same room, have different offices, alternate time arrangement in the same space, etc.?

The benefits of working at home together: we are at home together, all day every day. The challenges of working at home together: we are at home together, all day every day! A solution to the above benefits and challenges: we have separate offices.

Q: How do you make working from home work when you travel? Do you travel and take your work with you in all seasons or just when the weather is nice and warm? Is flexibility a major reason why you chose to work from home – work, scheduling, vacation, etc. flexibility?

When we travel, we take our work with us, any time of year. We consider ourselves very fortunate to be able to work from anywhere in the world. We also contact current and potential clients wherever we travel. This ensures almost all travel we do are business trips and is a great way to get to know the area as we are meeting with locals. It is also a wonderful way to get new clients as we have learned!

Flexibility is a major reason of why we choose to work from home. We both have an entrepreneurial spirit and prefer to be our own bosses. No work clothes, no traffic, no filling up the vehicle with gas, no worries about extra dollars for parking, coffee, lunches, etc.

Q: What are the unique advantages and disadvantages to working from home in rural Alberta? Do you use any off-the-grid or alternative energy sources as your primary or backup power systems?

The unique advantages to working from home in a rural setting are that it is quiet and can be an inexpensive place to live and work. The unique disadvantages to remote work in a rural setting include the possibility that internet may be intermittent and cell phone coverage can be spotty. We also have a generator for backup power.

Q: Is there any specific advice or suggestions you would give to those who work from home or want to work from home while living in a rural setting or a remote area?

Our advice and suggestions for living in a rural setting are:
- To be prepared for power outages.
- That roads may not be passable and without a corner store or office supply store 5 minutes away, it is important to stock up on essentials!
- Get to know your neighbors. Be kind to them and treat them with respect — you will need their help someday and they will probably need your help, too.

One must be able to prioritize, close the office door and ignore the dirty dishes, laundry, pets that want your attention, favorite TV programs, Facebook, personal phone calls or anything else that arises. Make sure to set goals, both personal and professional ones. Write them down and revisit them occasionally. One would be surprised how many goals are achieved just by knowing what they are and having a plan on how to reach them.

The lines between co-workers and husband and wife can be blurred. Communication is most important to keep the relationship and company successful. All aspects of both business and personal must be able to be communicated and listened to, in order for both people to feel there is a healthy balance. I (Natalie) think it is essential that both people know about both corporate and personal finances including sales, revenue, debt, cash flow, etc. so there are no secrets (nor any surprises). This communication has helped keep our aging account receivable and bad debt to a minimum. For instance, I collect the outstanding accounts and keep Rolf apprised of who and how much is owing. If a client does not pay on time, then Rolf will call him and collect the money. Rolf has built a friendly relationship with all of our clients so the clients find it difficult to ignore him or to say 'no' we are not paying.

Other times, not communicating about the business is essential, like when having dinner! When communication does not work and a decision needs to be made, then there must be one person who makes the final decision. This person should be decided early on in the company existence. Both of us bring a different skill set to the company. I enjoy the paperwork and finance side of things and am detailed oriented, whereas Rolf is a great salesman and enjoys dealing with the clients. Therefore, for us, it is more of a collaboration than a co-worker situation. However, when an impasse arises (which has happened once in 17 years), Rolf gets the final say.

We have an understanding that each person may require their own space for a while, which may mean going to read in a corner undisturbed or going to visit family in Vancouver for a weekend.

And finally: be honest, be fair and if you work hard, you will be rewarded.

Heather Spontak and Kadin Goldberg: Artists Working from Home While on the Road in the United States

Photo of Heather Spontak, a potter, decorating a cup.
Photo credit: Heather Spontak/Kadin Goldberg.

Photo of Kadin Goldberg, a Plein Air painter, painting outdoors.
Photo credit: Claire M. Reitz Photography

Interview with Heather Spontak (www.heatherspontak.com), a potter, and Kadin Goldberg (www.kadingoldberg.com), a Plein Air painter, artists who create and sell their work while traveling on the road throughout the United States. Heather and Kadin provide insight into what it takes (hint: being well organized and lots of planning helps!) to work from home while on the road.

Heather Spontak Bio:

Heather Spontak is a Potter originally from upstate New York and has since lived in various parts of the Southeast and Midwest. As a student she studied ceramics abroad at Studio Art Centers International in Florence, Italy, and in 2012 she received her BFA from East Tennessee State University. From 2013-2016 she worked as a Resident Artist at Odyssey Clay-Works in Asheville, NC. Heather enjoys hiking, knitting, and playing the ukulele. She is currently traveling throughout the United States with her cat, dog and mobile pottery studio.

Kadin Goldberg Bio:

Kadin Goldberg is a landscape painter from the Rocky Mountains of south-central Montana. After graduating from the University of Montana, Missoula with a B.A. in Psychology, he decided to pursue his childhood passion of art. He studied portrait and figure drawing at the Angel Academy of Art in Florence, Italy, and continued his studies at Angela Cunningham's Fine Art Studio in North Carolina. While primarily a self-taught painter, his technical training in traditional drawing techniques informs his current body of work. Today Kadin travels throughout the United States painting "en plein air" and enjoys reading, playing guitar and hiking.

Q: What is it like working from home on the road, traveling, as artists? Do you adjust your working hours based on whether you are traveling on the road or staying in one location for a longer time?

Our "studio" takes many forms. We joke that all Kadin needs is a backpack, which is pretty much the case but not entirely true. Kadin is a Plein Air painter meaning he works primarily outdoors so he can paint a scene directly. He goes hiking to a certain location and paints for several hours. Occasionally he refines the piece back at home. At camp, Heather has a small table and pottery wheel for working underneath our awning or if the weather isn't quite right, she will occasionally rent studio space. For firing she rents kiln space from different community clay centers. Working from home on the road for us has been quite liberating but has also come with its own set of challenges.

Traveling full time as artists on the road is quite different from when we had our own studio. The biggest differences are a certain dependency on weather conditions and space for storage. Our work schedule is mainly based around when we have events coming up and if the weather is good for working outdoors. It's nearly impossible to keep a set schedule of hours so instead we work hard when the weather is nice and take it easy when the wind is howling outside.

Q: Do you have a different way of or unique approach to marketing and promoting yourselves as artists while on the road compared to when you were based out of Red Lodge, Montana?

As far as marketing and promotion are concerned, there isn't a huge difference in how we market our work living on the road vs having a physical studio. Kadin participates in Plein Air events, has an active Patreon page, and sells online. Heather participates in craft shows and at local farmers markets. Living on the road has made it so that we are able to do different events and meet a lot of lovely people, but it isn't all that different than how we were selling work back in Montana.

Q: What do you find has been the most helpful and important...

...advice that you have received for your on-the-road business?

The best advice we have received is to trust that things will work out. There are countless times this idea has been proven both for us as well as for other friends. Making a living as an Artist really is like riding a wave. There are times when everything happens all at once and times when nothing is going on at all. Trusting that there is always another wave coming is really crucial.

...strategy in running a business successfully while on the road?

Our strategy for running our businesses and really in general in life is to be really intentional with what we need. We spend money on quality things that will last and do as much as we can ourselves. Staying organized and spending enough time planning are also key. Our schedule of events is planned about 6-8 months in advance which helps keep the workflow organized. Learning to keep good financial records has been really important. It has taken us some time to figure out the right system but finding an easy way to keep organized is essential.

*Heather and Kadin working on their art
while traveling around the United States.
Photo credit: Heather Spontak/Kadin Goldberg.*

*The current van and trailer, home of artists Heather and Kadin while
traveling around the United States as they work and live while on the
road. Photo credit: Heather Spontak/Kadin Goldberg*

Angela Lockert: A Pediatric Nurse Practitioner and Mom Working from Home in Alberta, Canada

Photo of Angela Lockert, a pediatric nurse practitioner and mom of two working from home in Calgary. Photo credit: Angela Lockert

Photo of Angela Lockert's home office space and the view from her work area. Photo credit: Angela Lockert

Interview with Angela Lockert, a pediatric nurse practi-tioner with a focus in child and youth mental health, and mom of two children, who is working from home in Calgary. Angela shares about the transition to remote work due to Covid-19 (in March 2020) and how she makes it work for her family, and gives tips and encouragement to moms working from home and those considering it.

Q: As a paediatric nurse practitioner, what was the transition like going from working in a hospital setting to working from home? When did you first begin working from home due to Covid-19?

Prior to COVID-19 I was working within a clinic setting as a mental health nurse consultant, seeing children and adoles-cents in person who were struggling with their mental health, and seeking psychiatric support. When Covid hit (March 2020), our clinic stopped seeing patients in person, and we moved to a virtual platform (Zoom). This was challenging initially as we needed to ensure the virtual platform was secure (due to the highly sensitive nature of the topics we discuss). There was also a transition time getting everyone comfortable with tech-nology (having working speakers, ensuring their cameras were turned on, and computers/internet working properly). As time went on, we also noted that it was challenging for some children and adolescents to meet virtually versus in person and we needed to change the process of the meeting to include "break out rooms" so the child/adolescent could meet in a separate chat room with one professional to talk about their concerns versus everyone in the chat room.

Q: As a mom, how do you make remote work feasible? What have been some of the benefits and challenges to working from home?

Without my husband being able to care for the children, I

would not have been able to work from home and watch the children at the same time. Due to the risk of having our 2- and 4-year-old in a highly busy daycare setting with Covid, we pulled our children out of daycare, and my husband has taken a leave from his job to watch the children. This has given me the ability to focus on the work I need to do with my job. I do love being able to work from home as I don't have to drive to and from work every day, and I can wake up and start my day. It's nice having the ability to have breakfast and lunch as a family, and I find that I see my children a lot more than when they were in daycare.

Some challenges of working from home is that the house can become quite loud when the dogs are barking, the children are having tantrums, and I am trying to work. I have found that putting my headphones and listening to music helps or having my headphones on when I am in a meeting.

Q: Looking ahead, do you plan to continue working remotely? Why or why not?

As the case numbers continue to rise here in Alberta, I think that everyone will have to continue working from home, if able, to help prevent the spread until there is a vaccine. Some of our patients do not do well on a virtual platform, and we have had to move them back to in person ensuring Covid precautions are in place. I would love to in the future, see a balance between working from home, and working in the office. I do miss visiting with my colleagues, and having our team together.

Q: What suggestions and tips can you share to encourage moms who either already work from home or who are thinking about working from home?

It is important to have an office space that is relatively quiet, and has a door. Putting on headphones can help quiet the noise in the home, and ensuring that your door is locked when you have important meetings that should not be disrupted. Being able to work from home saves time in terms of avoiding the commute to and from work. Always practice self-care as being a mom and working from home are two full-time jobs. Be patient with yourself.

Dorothy Mazeau: A Look at HomeSharing and Working from Home in Ontario, Canada

Photo of Dorothy Mazeau, a long-time community advocate, retired architect and practicing realtor in Ontario. Founder of Golden HomeSharing Connections and its online database, Golden Girls Canada. Photo credit: Lisa Piellusch of Picture Your Life Photography.

Photo of Dorothy Mazeau's home office space, which includes a keyboard. Photo credit: Dorothy Mazeau

Interview with Dorothy Mazeau, a long-time community advocate, retired architect and practising realtor based in Ontario. As a realtor specializing in working with seniors, she realizes that there is a need for a wider range of living options for her clients, especially those who are looking for an alternative to currently available solutions.

Drawing on her own experience of living in shared homes for more than 20 years, Dorothy founded Golden HomeSharing Connections (www.goldengirlscanada.ca) and its online database Golden Girls Canada as a way to help others learn about the benefits of this way of life and find compatible home-mates. As well as the database, the website provides members with links to live workshops, webinars, and helpful information to guide them on their journey to creating a shared home.

Q: You founded Golden Girls Canada and Golden Home-Sharing Connections in 2017 to provide home sharing as another housing option to mature adults. How do home sharing and working from home combine – do these two lifestyle options work well together?

Every situation is different. There is no reason home sharing and working from home cannot work well together, as long as the household has reached an understanding on how it will be handled. The simplest way is for each household member to have their own dedicated, private office space. Adequate broadband width for internet access is also essential, especially if more than one household member works from home.

If totally separate space is not available in the house and only the household member who works from home is at home during the day, that can work too. During these days of Covid, the issues of home-sharers working from home is very similar to those in any family where the adults are all working from home. Not easy! But manageable if they can hammer out a schedule that works for all of them.

Q: How do you schedule your work from home hours when living in a home share? How can scheduled work events such as webinars and online meetings fit with the shared living areas? How would they be coordinated? What advice do you have for others?

I have been working from home for much of the past 20 years, in various shared homes. For the most part, I have had my own dedicated office space, and could work whenever I needed to — sometimes long into the night!

Generally, I have been the only one home during the day, however there was a period when two of us were working at home in an "open concept" house. While we each had office space in the basement, it was an unfinished space that we used mostly for files and supply storage — it wasn't that pleasant! So, we both ended up working with our laptops on opposite ends of the dining room table! Fortunately, there was one front room with a door that could be closed; we used that room for private phone calls or online meetings — making sure to coordinate use well ahead of time, so our scheduled use didn't overlap!

Currently I live in a home where I have the lower level almost entirely for my own use. I use a dining room table as my office desk, and have a couple of spots where I can set up for a Zoom meeting or video recording, with portable lighting that I can move from one space to another. If I am scheduling a workshop or recording session, I alert my two home-mates, so they know not to disturb me. Fortunately, the house is big enough that noise is not an issue.

My advice for anyone considering working from home in a new shared situation is to include among your "must haves" a dedicated, private office space, away from the noise and activity of the rest of the household. That will be one deciding factor in whether to enter into a home-sharing agreement.

Most home-based businesspeople, other than personal

service providers, such as operating a hair salon or medical office, do not meet with their clients or customers in their home. If that is an essential part of your business make sure that your home-mates can accept that, and also make sure that your household insurance covers business use — you may need to pay the difference if your rate goes up significantly. But it will be worth the cost if a claim arises!

Q: What skills and experience do mature adults bring that help them make the adjustment to remote work? What challenges have you faced working from home and how did you overcome them?

Anyone working from home needs to be a disciplined, self-directed individual. If you work for a larger company, obviously the company will likely have its own requirements and ways of monitoring how you are spending your work-time. If you are self-employed, you need to be your own taskmaster. That being said, it's easy to find yourself absorbed by work during all your waking hours!

In order to guard against burn-out, be sure to schedule time for fun in your life and for social time with your home-mates—which can include helping with meal prep and doing the dishes. One of the lovely benefits of home-sharing is that household tasks can be shared. You won't be on "dinner duty" every night, but you also need to take your turn. And of course, if you occasionally need to beg off duty to meet a work deadline, be sure to pick up the slack somewhere else. Home-sharing is all about give-and-take.

And remember to include "alone time," too! Don't feel guilty about taking a nap or reading a book or taking a walk. You need to be kind to yourself in order to be kind to anyone else.

Trish Tutton: Speaker and Mindfulness Teacher Based in Alberta, Canada

An Interview on my blog (www.barborigarnet.com/blog) originally posted on May 20, 2020 — As a result of Covid-19, many people and business owners had to quickly transition to working from home and remote working. Today, I am happy to have Trish Tutton (www.trishtutton.com/), a Speaker and Mindfulness Teacher based in Banff, Alberta, share about her transition in March 2020 to working from home:

Trish Tutton, Speaker and Mindfulness Teacher, and her home office space. Photo credit: Trish Tutton (www.trishtutton.com)

Q: How did you make the transition to leading yoga and meditation classes online? Was it a sudden change? Did you have some systems already in place to transition online?

When I started to see the increase in social distancing measures, I began realizing that I didn't feel comfortable teaching in person any longer [because of the possibility of the virus affecting my students or myself]. It was a quick decision, as things were changing rapidly.

Within a few days I saw other teachers moving to online classes and I really realized that folks are in need of these practices more than ever with the increasing stress and anxiety that was happening. I stopped teaching physical classes on Sunday, March 15, 2020, and began offering virtual ones by Wednesday, March 18. I had never taught a yoga class or a corporate mindfulness session virtually, only ever in person! I knew of Zoom and decided to hop on quickly and figure it out. I realized my services as a yoga teacher and corporate wellness consultant would be in need more than ever.

Q: Going forward, will you continue to lead classes online?

Absolutely — along with teaching yoga I also am a speaker and make most of my living speaking at conferences and meetings about how to manage stress and work happier with mindfulness. All of my spring conferences have been cancelled, but luckily, I've been doing some more virtual work in that capacity with businesses who want to support their employees' mental health. I've been teaching yoga and running these webinar sessions online and I will continue to do so until the restrictions open up and allow us to gather in person again. It's a pleasure to continue to do what I do even in a virtual capacity.

Q: What opportunities and challenges do you think will be faced in the future by businesses and entrepreneurs in remote work?

Being in the corporate wellness world I find it interesting that I've seen a lot of talk about how to boost employee productivity at home, how to help employees set up a home office, etc. I think the biggest challenge for companies right now is helping their employees manage their fears and feelings around the pandemic! These fears are actually the biggest threat to a person's productivity, in the end. I think the opportunity companies have right now is to find ways to bring their team together while supporting their health and well-being, so that they can have a positive influence on productivity, morale, and well-being. I've had the great pleasure to work with several companies on wellness initiatives during the pandemic and we're seeing huge boosts in morale and positivity in light of this challenging pandemic. The truth is that this isn't the first stressful event we've encountered and it won't be the last. Helping your team navigate this challenging time will only set you up for more success in the future.

Debbie Boehlen: Offering Health & Wellness Courses Online from Nova Scotia, Canada

Debbie Boehlen's well-organized office space. Debbie Boehlen, founder of the Canadian Centre of Indian Head Massage, has outfitted her office with lots of drawers, providing a place to put papers and supplies. In addition, her work area has plenty of desk space and a ledge on which her computer, speakers, a jar of pens, and a lamp sit. Photo credit: Debbie Boehlen (www.indianheadmassagecanada.com).

Interview with Debbie Boehlen, who founded the Canadian Centre of Indian Head Massage (www.indianheadmassagecanada.com) in 2003 and has been a holistic practitioner and instructor of several modalities since that time. She has been offering in-class training, traveling through-out Canada, in Indian Head Massage, Rejuvenating Face Massage, Ayurvedic Foot Massage, Usui Reiki, Axiatonal Alignment, and Animal Reiki. She has also offered sessions in these modalities and several others such as Reflexology and IonCleanse.

In 2017 she began to offer online training and now provides this training for all three forms of massage she teaches. Debbie has worked from her home office for the past 18 years.

Q: Can you share when you began offering online courses. In what ways has offering courses online — in Indian Head Massage, Ayurvedic Foot Massage, and Rejuvenating Face Massage — changed your business?

I began to offer online courses in 2017. It has made the courses I offer more easily available for many who would otherwise not be able to attend. It has meant less travel time and expense for both myself and the students, and a reduction in the cost of course materials as all information is available within the online course. Students are encouraged to keep a copy of the course notes and videos. Because of the reduced cost of expenses, I was able to reduce the cost of the online course, which is exactly the same course as the one offered in-class. I have had a lot of positive feedback about the online courses, the only downfall is that I don't have as much contact with students as I did when I only taught in person.

Q: What steps did you take to create online courses? Did you need any help in creating the content such as recording and uploading videos, updating e-commerce or online payment systems, or any other aspect? Has the prep-

aration of the online courses been challenging?

I updated my course manuals and uploaded the theoretical information, the same information available in the in-class course. I researched and found a course hosting site that was easy to use for both myself and the students. I did not need help to create content since it is the same content as the in-class courses I have been offering for the past 18 years but I did need help in recording the videos and I hired someone to edit and upload the videos. The course hosting site I use has an easy-to-use payment system built right in. I would say the first course was challenging as it was the first time I was doing anything like this but the subsequent two courses were not as challenging. It was time-consuming however for all three courses to be created and uploaded.

Q: Have there been any changes to municipal or other government rules and regulations – or insurance requirements - with regards to your business now that you offer online courses?

To my knowledge no, there have been no changes though some associations may not recognize online courses as they do in-class ones. Covid-19 has been a catalyst for change and I am seeing more and more courses being offered, or being considered to be offered online. One association that I am familiar with has recently sent out a questionnaire asking its members how they feel about online training in that particular modality. Up until now, it was strictly in-class only as per their by-laws.

Q: How has your business made it through Covid-19? What challenges have you encountered and overcome and what successes have you had?

With the shutdown and inability to teach or offer sessions in-person my business suffered greatly as I was not able to work as I have always done. But at the same time, I have had a greater number of online registrations. Many who took and are continuing to take the online courses have been at home with time on their hands and decided to pursue studies, that some just never had the time to do. With travel restrictions and safety measures in place, it has been easier for students to study from home, at their pace.

Photos of Work-from-Home Spaces:
Alberta author Fran Kimmel's home office space

Alberta-based writer and author Fran Kimmel's writing and home office space. Fran has natural light coming into her office space through the windows, a fireplace to keep warm with and keep her working space cozy throughout the colder months, plenty of desk space and bookshelves, and a couch to relax on for a well-deserved break.

Fran has lots of bookshelf space for the books she needs to refer to as she works on her writing. In addition to books on the shelves, Fran also has some quotes, an artwork, and photos of family and friends to help personalize and make the space her own while also keeping her inspired and encouraged to work on her writing to reach her goals.

Photo credits: Fran Kimmel (www.frankimmel.com).

Photo of Fran Kimmel. Photo credit: Monique de St. Croix.

Kristi Durette's, Associate Vice President of Institutional Advancement at Southern New Hampshire University (SNHU), home office space

Then (home office in 2018)...

Now (home office in 2020)...

Photo credits: Kristi Durette.

A lot can change in two years and especially since in the last year, working from home has become the norm for many. Kristi Durette, Associate Vice President of Institutional Advancement at Southern New Hampshire University (SNHU), shows what her home office looked like in 2018 and what it looks like now in 2020. Both spaces feature a very well-organized space with room on the table to spread out needed papers, books, and supplies, allowing her to completely focus on work tasks when she works from home. Kristi has lots of light, both natural and artificial light.

In the first two photos, she has a very nice artwork to complete her inspiring work-from-home space. In the 2020 photo, Kristi has expanded her table space and work area by adding another table to her home office.

Author of this book, Barbori Garnet's work-from-home spaces

Photo of Barbori Garnet's (the author's) work-from-home spaces since 2016.

In the top photo, my work space includes natural light streaming in through the window and artificial light from the lamp on the desk, a chair to sit on while working or alternately to stand while working, ivy plants which add a touch of greenery, enough desk space

for a phone and a few papers, and artwork on the wall to the left. This wonderfully light-filled corner was made possible by removing a corner gas fireplace and moving the window five feet from the middle of the wall.

Photos taken by the author, Barbori Garnet.

In the second photo, my work space also has natural light coming in through a couple of windows along with a small table lamp, a wooden chair with a seat pillow (not pictured), an ivy plant in the background, desk space enough for pens, pencils, and watercolor brushes, and a shelf behind the desk to hold binders, books, and papers.

My work spaces have each been a different size and in different parts of a room. However, I have had dedicated work areas as well as space for the supplies and materials I need at hand. I am able to work with the spaces I have to create a home office and continue doing work I enjoy.

By reading the interviews which were presented above in **Part 2: Extraordinary People Who Work from Home**, my hope is that you draw encouragement, inspiration, and new ideas for your remote work journey. When you face challenges, discouragement, or disappointment in your work or business, you can read these interviews and be reminded that everyone encounters trying times at some time or other but the important thing is to remain optimistic, adapt to current circumstances, and try new things.

Here is a summary of the key points shared by the interviewees.

Summary of Highlights and Wisdom Gained from Interviews with Home-Based Business Owners and Employees
- Importance of being self-disciplined
- Importance of technology and having an organized, well-equipped home office
- Finding a niche for your business and identifying needs of potential clients
- Time
  o Flexibility of work hours
  o Commute time used more effectively
  o More time available to spend with family
- Importance of spouse/family support

Part 3

Hands-on Workbook:
Is Remote Work Right for You?

Part 3 presents questions for you to answer. The questions are grouped into categories including: *Setting Up Your Workspace, A Way of Life – Your Work Day, Socialization and Support Systems, Technology*, and *Visualization and Goals.* By taking the time to write down answers to these questions, you will get to know yourself better. You will also develop a better understanding of the strengths you already bring to working from home and the challenges you may face as you get ready to set up your work space and begin to work remotely.

Setting Up Your Workspace

If you do not currently have a home office/work space set up and ready to use, take the time to think about the possible areas of your home where you could have one. Some suggestions and ideas include:
- In the corner of a living room
- In a den or bedroom
- A stair landing
- Under stairs area
- Entrance hall
- A closet
- Enclosed porch or sun room, etc.
- A bump out

Write down any ideas that come to mind for possible spaces to convert and use as a home office:

Are there any changes or improvements you need to make to your work space at home? If yes, write them down in the space below:

    a.   Change to be made –

    Complete by:

    b.   Change to be made –

    Complete by:

    c.   Change to be made –

    Complete by:

What are ways in which you can personalize your work space at home? Write your ideas down here:

1.

2.

3.

Look through a few home styling or home interior magazines or books (Small Homes, House Beautiful, House and Home, to name a few) to find examples of and inspiration for home office spaces. Make notes on which features you like and se- lect those elements which you could add to your own work space to make it even better and more inspiring.

A) Draw the layout/floorplan of your work/home office space the way it is now:

B) Now, draw the layout/floorplan of your *perfect* work/ home office space:

C) Is there any change you can make to the current layout to make it closer to your perfect layout? If so, what is the change and how soon can you make the change?

A Way of Life: Your Work Day

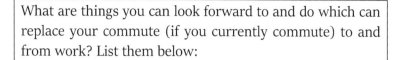

What are things you can look forward to and do which can replace your commute (if you currently commute) to and from work? List them below:

What part(s) of the day are you most productive and work best at? Circle the time(s) of the day when you work best:

    a) Early morning: 6 a.m. – 9 a.m.
    b) Morning: 9 a.m. – 12 p.m.
    c) Early afternoon: 12 p.m. – 2 p.m.
    d) Afternoon: 2 p.m. – 5 p.m.
    e) Early evening: 5 p.m. – 7 p.m.
    f) Evening: 7 p.m. – 10 p.m.
    g) Late evening: 10 p.m. – 2 a.m.
    h) Wee morning: 2 a.m. – 6 a.m.

What are ways you can streamline and be more efficient in your work?

Are there any lifestyle changes you may need to make before or while beginning to work from home, such as getting enough sleep, drinking more water, or getting in more exercise?

Do the above changes you would need to make affect you and your decision to work from home?

Describe — in as much detail as possible — your ideal work day. Some ideas and questions to get you started are: What kind of tasks are you working at? Are you meeting with clients and if yes, how many and at what time?

Socialization and Support Systems

Brainstorm some ways to better get to know family members. How can you spend time with them in ways that allow you to get to know them more:

A) Write down what you like about interacting with colleagues at the office:

B) Brainstorm some ideas for ways to better get to know colleagues you might work with virtually:

What are some ways that family and friends can help out at home (even things which they ought to stop doing for example, stomping loudly when walking up and down the stairs) or elsewhere, so that working from home would be a success for you? Write it below and share it with family and friends:

Who is your cheer group (i.e., those who support, encourage, listen, and provide feedback) from amongst your family and friends? Write the names of five people who are your cheer group, how they support you, and what you appreciate about them:

1. Name:

Support provided:

Appreciate that:

2. Name:

Support provided:

Appreciate that:

3. Name:

Support provided:

Appreciate that:

4. Name:

Support provided:

Appreciate that:

5. Name:

Support provided:

Appreciate that:

Write down your team of professionals, including their name and contact information:

Accountant
Name:

Contact:

Insurance - Personal
Name:

Contact:

Insurance - Business
Name:

Contact:

Computer Specialist
Name:

Contact:

<u>Lawyer</u>
Name:

Contact:

<u>Doctor</u>
Name:

Contact:

<u>Dentist</u>
Name:

Contact:

<u>Carpenter/Handyman</u>
Name:

Contact:

<u>Plumber</u>
Name:

Contact:

Auto Mechanic
Name:

Contact:

Technology

What technology do you already have available and ready to use for remote work? List the items below:
for ex. – Acer laptop
- Canon camera
- HP printer (model)
-
-
-

A) Which technology will you need to upgrade or replace in the next three to five years? What is the estimated cost?

B) How much are you saving each month to make the above upgrades and purchases, without going into debt or using as little credit as possible?

I am saving/putting aside $___ each month so that I have cash on hand for any necessary upgrades and purchases in order to remain debt-free and/or continue working from home.

Maintaining your technological equipment and keeping it in tip-top shape is important to remote work success. Write down below the dates that you need to renew software and have regular maintenance done:

Security/Virus software - renewal date:

Computer maintenance schedule:

Other important dates to remember:

What technology skills do you need to learn or upgrade?

Which resources — books, courses, videos — will you access to acquire the technology skills you need?

Visualization and Goals

Visualize and describe your ideal before-work and after-work routines:

What are your goals, both short-term and long-term, in working from home?

Short-term goals in working from home...

Long-term goals in working from home...

What are your goals in life (personal, travel, financial, etc.), both short-term and long-term?

Short-term life goals...

Long-term life goals...

How often do you currently write down your goals? How often do you review/revisit your goals to make sure that you are on track to reach them or to note any changes to your vision?

What decisions, actions, and steps will you take to help you reach your goals?

For example, will you save a certain amount of money each month to buy a property, are you going to register for and attend a workshop, or will you check in on a regular basis with a mentor in order to keep yourself accountable to your goals?

What are ways you will relax and recharge (e.g., reading, writing, taking a nap, exercising, getting a massage) when not working on your goals?

With **Part 3: Hands-on Workbook: Is Remote Work Right for You?** now completed, you have considered many topics important in working from home: your work and life goals, strengths, and ideal routine and work area. Remember these insights as you prepare to take and seek to implement the next step in your work from home journey.

By reading through all of *Home at the Office: Working Remotely as a Way of Life*, you have not only learned a lot about working remotely but also about yourself. Keep in mind and apply the knowledge you have gained along the way. As you find or create the remote work position that is right for you, may you treasure the gift of working from home and the beginning of your enjoyment of freedom, flexibility, and independence. I wish you all the best in working remotely as a way of life.

Notes
Working from Home: A Way of Life
1. Shepherd, Maddie. 2020. "28 Surprising Working From Home Statistics." *Fundera*. https://www.fundera.com/resources/working-from-home-statistics.
2. St. Denis, Jen. 2020. "Nearly 5 million more Canadians are working from home, and many like it: survey." *CTV News Vancouver*. https://bc.ctvnews.ca/nearly-5-million-more-canadians-are-working-from-home-and-many-like-it-surveys-1.4903045.

Appendix A - Articles

Working from Home on the Farm and Homestead

By Barbori Garnet

Working from home has its own set of challenges but even so, the positives far outweigh the negatives. Remote work from a homestead or farm can bring a family together, build resiliency, and provide many streams of income. Whether you are just beginning to work or have been working at a home-based business for a long time, here are the many benefits to making the decision to work from home.

Family Ties

Working from home on the farm can benefit the whole family. Different generations can interact and learn from one another along with assisting in different aspects of the family enterprise. A business run from the farm can involve everyone, giving parents the chance to show the day-to-day operations of their work while letting children see the various tasks their parents do to operate a business.

It can also permit one partner to stay home with the children while the other partner works on the business. Steve Maxwell, *Harrowsmith's* Home and Design editor and owner of Bailey Line Road based on Manitoulin Island, Ontario, was happy to share some of the advantages of working from home, "For me, it's all benefits. The last time I had a regular 'job' was 1989, and since then I've been working exclusively from my homestead creating and selling articles, videos and online courses. My income has allowed my wife to follow her dream of staying home and it has also allowed our five kids to grow up with two parents at home all the time. I look forward to my work every day".

The Gig Economy

Making a living at working from home means that the products or services you offer are something that people need and want to purchase. It is important, too, to have multiple sources of income coming in. Maxwell confirms this importance, adding, "For people like me, it's an exciting challenge earning a living for a family without any guarantees. In 30 years, it has consistently worked out fine. Part of the reason is that all working-from-home businesses should have multiple streams of income." If one stream slows down, you will still have other sources which are bringing in money. In setting up multiple income streams in this "gig economy", entrepreneurs know the value of creating digital downloads of e-books, video tutorials, Zoom online workshops, writing for related publications, consulting or coaching.

The Secrets of Success (are not secrets at all)

Farmers and homesteaders are well aware that the care and upkeep of their property takes time, perseverance, and non-stop work. Running a home-based business is no different and demands the same elements. On what it takes to find success in working from home, Steve Maxwell states, "Success working from any kind of home involves diligently applying skills that surprisingly few people seem willing or able to exercise. You need to set your own schedule, fix your own computer and gear, sell your services, deal with clients, look after payments, and brainstorm creative ideas that the world is willing to pay for. People who already earn money farming probably have these skills, so the transition to working from the farm digitally will probably be easier".

Despite the long hours, there's a distinct advantage in setting your own schedule and eliminating the commute. Dedication and a willingness to try new things and adjust as needed are part of the keys to successfully working remotely.

Resiliency

By developing a business which allows you to work remotely from your homestead, you can secure a place to withstand economic changes as most recently encountered during the Covid-19 pandemic. "The C-19 event has reminded me how valuable it is to be able to earn a living from our homestead," Maxwell says. "There's been no significant change in our life here, except for two university-age kids coming home. The ability to earn money digitally from the farm is part of a larger theme of self-reliance that we've put into practice here since 1989. My two university boys who are back home now are also earning money online while doing their schooling online too. One is writing articles for clients in the U.S., and the other is doing medical research and video analysis."

Generating a consistent income will become increasingly vital to withstand any up and down changes that the economy may bring. Having a successful home-based business can offer more control over income and stability, provided cautious financial measures are in place.

Making money through a home-based business is extremely rewarding. Yes, it is up to the individual to make all the decisions regarding work hours, finding clients, and items to sell. However, working from home on the farm and homestead gives you the opportunity to diversify and maximize your income, the independence to be resilient when facing unforeseen economic circumstances, and the time to spend with your family.

Originally published in Harrowsmith Magazine's 2021 Fall Almanac. Reprinted with permission from Harrowsmith Magazine. Photo credit: Jules Torti.

The Writer's Home Office: Setting Goals for Your Writing Space
By Barbori Garnet

Setting goals for your home office space first will help you to be more focused and efficient in your writing time. By setting goals such as when and how long you will write for, how often you will tidy and organize your work space, when you will practice reading your writing, and perhaps decide on inviting over others to hear you read your work, will result in spending your time writing and growing in your writing path at your home office.

How much time do you want to spend writing and working away in your space? The answer to this question will be based in part on what your writing goals are — how many words or pages you want to write each day along with how soon you want to complete a story or project — and what your other time commitments are (family, work, volunteer, etc.). Once you know what your current commitments are and what you want to accomplish in your writing, then you will know how much time, and when, to set aside for writing in your home office.

Having decided on your writing time, consider setting aside time to read your work. Reading your own writing out loud is a great way to get familiar with the flow of the words you have written, know what is coming next in the story or chapter, and be comfortable with proper posture whether sitting or standing. Practicing reading your writing will prepare you for both virtual and in-person readings and increase your confidence and success.

Another goal to consider is whether you will invite people over to your writer's home office, using it as a literary salon. Invite writers as part of a writing group, or special guests who come to hear you read your work. As it is your writing space, it is important to go with what you feel comfortable with and what works best for you.

Setting goals and following through on keeping your writer's nook organized and tidy will help you to have a place you love to write in. Examples of goals to set include sorting and filing papers at the end of each day/week/month and having a calendar to record deadlines for projects/contests/submissions. It is important to have a place to note things to research/print/ write and to go through bookshelves to ensure that books and notebooks you refer to often are handy and close by. If you have a smaller place in which to write, you may have to get creative with storage solutions to keep your table free of clutter.

In addition to setting aside time to write and organizing your space, think about ways in which you can beautify your work area. Can you place an indoor plant, such as an ivy or peace lily, on a shelf or on the table? Could you treat yourself to a bouquet of flowers once a month? Or perhaps a seasonal wreath on a wall, door, or easel would add just the right touch of color, beauty, and personality. Giving some thought to ways in which to add cheer to your space will result in a more inviting and personal place for you to write in.

Before beginning to write, take the time to set goals for

your writing area. Having regular writing and reading times, knowing when and how often to tidy and organize, and adding elements of beauty and brightness to your writer's home office will make it an oasis where you enjoy writing.

Originally published in Opal Writers' Magazine's November 2020 digital magazine issue. Reprinted with permission from Opal Publishing. Photo from Pixabay.

The Writer's Home Office: A Festive Touch
By Barbori Garnet

With the Christmas and holiday season coming up, why not take the time to add a festive touch to your home office? Taking the time to play holiday music, decorate, or choose from any or all of the below ideas could be just the answer to making your writing area a home to the holidays.

Play Christmas or holiday music either before your writing time or softly in the background while you write. You can choose from instrumental music or songs with words. If you play a musical instrument, play a couple of songs for fun. Music can help a lot in setting the right mood or in providing needed inspiration for what to write. A favorite holiday song could trigger a memory which may inspire a story or article.

The holidays can be a great time to come up with new ideas for and write articles on topics related to holidays, whether Christmas, Easter or Thanksgiving. You may think of topics to write on such as the best flowers for the Christmas season, holiday side hustles, or navigating family visits during the holidays. The holidays are also a good time to think about and find which holiday-themed writing markets and contests you may wish to prepare for and enter.

Get outside for a walk, to cross-country, or perhaps to skate. While getting in some exercise and fresh air, take in the festive wreaths, red ribbons, and lights in your neighborhood or around the city. Notice the way the sun is reflected by the snow, the crunch-crunch sound of snow under your shoes as you walk, or the smooth glide of cross-country skis and skates. Let all of this inspire you and remember these sights and sounds when you go to write.

Decorate your home office space with ornaments, a garland, perhaps a small tree on your desk, indoor lights, and the like. Make your own decorations, display family favorites, or do a combination of the two. You might also like to take some photos of your decorations and then incorporate those photos into a future article you may write about your decorating for the season. Bringing a merry and bright look to your work area for the Christmas and holiday time will add a special feel.

Maybe the month of December calls for enjoying special snacks and drinks of the season. While you work or when you are taking a well-deserved break, have a cup of hot cocoa, hot cider or eggnog, gingerbread man cookies, candy cane or peppermint brownies. Or make and savor a favorite family holiday recipe.

Finally, you can also share a little bit of your festive home office with others, even if it is mostly virtual this season. One idea is to hold a virtual Christmas party with other writer friends and have a short reading, play an online game, or do a Secret Santa and send e-gift cards to your online party buddies. Showing your creativity to others in how you decorated your space could not only add to a great time of fun and connecting during the upcoming holiday season but also inspire others.

Try adding a festive touch to your home office, using some of the tips above, and enjoy a Christmas look and feel in your work area this holiday season. I wish you all the best this Christmas and holiday season and in your writing.

Originally published in Opal Writers' Magazine's December 2020 digital magazine issue. Reprinted with permission from Opal Publishing. Photo from Pixabay.

The Writer's Home Office: Keeping Records and Making Lists
By Barbori Garnet

With the New Year upon us, now is a good time to start keeping records or update them, organize the records and files you have, and make some lists. Starting the year off by being well organized will provide you with a solid base from which to approach and plan and be ready for whatever comes your way. Here are some suggestions to begin.

- SORT AND ORGANIZE: Take the time, whether a day or two or a week, to sort through and organize your files. Decide what you need to keep and what can be shredded or recycled. Do you need a new binder, folder, or Duo Tang for 2021 papers and receipts? In which area of your home office, or in which other place at home, and on which shelf or in which drawer are you going to house your files and folders? Doing this now will help set you up for success and start this year off having a place for everything and everything in its place.

- MAKE A LIST: Make a list of the things you want to do and accomplish — conferences and events you plan to attend, retreats you want to go to, and topics for articles, stories, and books you wish to write. On this list, you can also include which magazines and newspapers you would like to submit a query to and be published in for the coming year. Having a list of what you want to achieve will help you know what to focus your time on and keep you on track each week, month, and quarter of the year.

- RECORD KEEPING: At least at the end of each week or month, and ideally after every transaction, record every transaction of income and expenses (supplies purchased, any contests entered, editing, professional/association fees, and more) which come in and out of your account. Whether you choose to record transactions on paper or in an online spreadsheet such as Excel, doing this on a regular basis will make it much easier for you to be prepared come tax time and to know if you are within your budget, staying out of debt, or making a profit.

- TRACK YOUR TIME: If you want to track how much time and when you spend time on writing, make sure to record on your calendar your writing times. By taking note of this, you can tell if you are spending enough time writing to reach your goals or if you need to add more hours. You may also notice certain patterns. For example, you might learn when you usually write and are most productive — morning, afternoon, or evening — and can then perhaps adjust your schedule to guard that time as special for your writing work.

- MAINTENANCE SCHEDULES: Finally, keep a record of when you last had computer maintenance done and when you renewed or updated your internet security. This way, you will know when these things need to be checked and done again. Whether you keep this record in a document on your computer, handwrite it in a notebook, or keep this list by your calendar, choose a way and a place that works for you and reminds you of these tasks. Maintaining your technology is a key factor in accomplishing your writing goals.

There is no time like the beginning of a New Year to sort, review, and organize papers and files and make lists of your goals. By doing this now and at regular times each week and month, you will know where papers and files are located which are needed for you to stay on track throughout the year and what you need to work on to reach your goals.

Originally published in Opal Writers' Magazine's January 2021 digital magazine issue. Reprinted with permission from Opal Publishing. Photo from Pixabay.

Appendix B – Resources

Below is a list of resources — books, job search websites, online communities and groups, and more — to help you find the information, support, and encouragement you need as you create a work from home life which blends in with your family, lifestyle, and goals.

Books
There are many books to find and read on the various aspects of working from home and other topics related to working, business, career development, and more. Start with this list of books, with a range of published dates, to expand your knowledge, gain perspective, and learn new skills by putting into practice some of the suggestions:
- _It Doesn't Have to Be Crazy at Work_
- _Remote: Office Not Required_
- _Rework_
  all by Jason Fried and David Heinemeier Hansson
- _The Laptop Millionaire: How Anyone Can Escape the 9 to 5 and Make Money Online_ by Mark Anastasi
- _Multiple Streams of Internet Income: How Ordinary People Make Extraordinary Money Online_ by Robert G. Allen
- _There Is Life After College: What Parents and Students Should Know About Navigating School to Prepare for the Jobs of Tomorrow_ by Jeffrey J. Selingo
- _The 4-Hour Workweek: Escape 9 - 5, Live Anywhere, and Join the New Rich (Expanded and Updated)_ by Timothy Ferriss
- _The 10% Entrepreneur: Live Your Startup Dream Without Quitting Your Day Job_ by Patrick J. McGinnis
- _ECOpreneuring: Putting Purpose and the Planet before Profits_ by John Ivanko and Lisa Kivirist
- _Making a Living While Making a Difference: Conscious_

Careers in an Era of Interdependence by Melissa Everett
- *Make Yourself at Home: Design Your Space to Discover Your True Self* by Moorea Seal (in particular, I recommend reading through Chapter 4 titled *Home Office*)
- *Money-Making Mom: How Every Woman Can Earn More and Make a Difference* by Crystal Paine
- *The Comeback: How Today's Moms Reenter the Workplace Successfully* by Cheryl Casone
- *Careergasm: Find Your Way to Feel-Good Work* by Sarah Vermunt
- *The Freelance Mum: A flexible career guide for better work-life balance* by Annie Ridout
- *The End of Jobs: Money, Meaning and Freedom Without the 9-to-5* by Taylor Pearson
- *100 Side Hustles: Unexpected Ideas for Making Money Without Quitting Your Day Job* and other books by Chris Guillebeau
- *Great Pajama Jobs: Your Complete Guide to Working from Home* by Kerry Hannon
- *How to Survive Without a Salary: Learning How to Live the Conserver Lifestyle* by Charles Long
- *The Ultimate Guide to Remote Work: How to Grow, Manage, and Work with Remote Teams* by Wade Foster and the Zapier Team
- *Work Together Anywhere: A Handbook on Working Successfully for Individuals, Teams & Managers* by Lisette Sutherland & K. Janene-Nelson
- *Will Work from Home: Earn the Cash — Without the Commute* by Tory Johnson and Robyn Freedman Spizman

Books on Finances from the *Marketing and Finances* chapter
- *The 9 Steps to Financial Freedom: Practical and Spiritual Steps So You Can Stop Worrying* by Suze Orman
- *The Retirement Guide for 50+: Winning Strategies to Make Your Money Last a Lifetime* by Suze Orman

- *Suze Orman's Personal Financial Online Course*
- *Biblical Economics: A Commonsense Guide to Our Daily Bread* by R.C. Sproul Jr.
- *More Than Finances: A Design for Freedom* by Larry Burkett
- *Rich Dad, Poor Dad* by Robert Kiyosaki
- *The Rules of Wealth: A Personal Code for Prosperity and Plenty* by Richard Templar
- *The Canadian Guide to Will and Estate Planning: Everything You Need to Know Today to Protect Your Wealth and Your Family Tomorrow* by Douglas Gray and John Budd
- *Stop Working: Here's How You Can!* by Derek Foster
- *Stop Working Too: You Still Can!* by Derek Foster

Books on Essential Oils
- *Essential Oils pocket reference 8th edition* published by Life Science
- *The Complete Aromatherapy & Essential Oils Handbook for Everyday Wellness* by Nerys Purchon and Lora Cantele
- *French Aromatherapy: Essential Oil Recipes & Usage Guide* by Jen O'Sullivan
- *The Essential Oils Hormone Solution: Reclaim Your Energy and Focus and Lose Weight Naturally* by Dr. Mariza Snyder

Job Search Websites

Ziprecruiter.com: From my experience, I have found the response rate from employers and Human Resource managers to my applications on Ziprecruiter.com to be the highest. If your preference is to work remotely for a company, I recommend starting your search on this site.

Glassdoor.com/.ca: This site lists jobs and positions but in addition, it also is a platform for employees to give reviews of their time working for employers.

FlexJobs.com: When searching on this site, you have the

option of finding a job based on 100% telecommuting, mostly telecommuting, etc.; field of work; full-time, part-time, or seasonal; and more. There are lots of positions to be found here.

PeoplePerHour.com: On this site, you can submit proposals for consideration for jobs and projects which people post. The projects range from Social Media to Creative Arts and from Writing to Tutoring. Another avenue for finding and landing work from home work!

FlexProfessionals.com: While this website lists jobs which require employees to do some part of work in either the Virginia, Washington, D.C., and New Jersey areas, it is a great website with great jobs in Public Relations, Bookkeeping, Administration, etc. A very well-organized website to certainly check out!

Indeed.com/.ca: Searching for work-from-home positions on this site means having just the right search word(s) so that both the job titles and job descriptions would line up to the type of work you are looking for.

LiveMusicTutor.com: If you teach a musical instrument or voice, you can teach online to students anywhere around the world. To be listed on this site as a music teacher, you first need to successfully complete LiveMusicTutor.com's application steps. Happy teaching!

HigherEdJobs.com: This website has a good assortment of online jobs at the college and university level for both academic and non-academic positions.

Online Communities and Groups

Nomad List (https://nomadlist.com/): Nomad List provides lots of helpful information to remote workers including providing ratings on what it is like to live and work in cities and countries around the world, remote job listings, coworking spaces, meetups, and more.

Digital Nomad Girls (https://digitalnomadgirls.com/): For those whose work allows them the ability to travel and work remotely from anywhere around the world, this website is a good place to find community as well as support, encouragement, and advice.

The Female Factor (https://www.femalefactor.global/): This website provides opportunities to grow as a leader and in your career, find mentors, and be part of events.

Other Online Communities and Groups:
- We Work Remotely (https://weworkremotely.com/)
- Run by Cam Woodsum - Remote Work Hub (https://remoteworkhub.com/)
- Freedom Is Everything (https://www.freedomiseverything.com/)

Additional Resources and Solutions

Your alma mater: If you graduated from college or university, take a look at your alma mater's online job board to see what is available. Or, speak to a Career Advisor who specializes in finding work-from-home openings for their students and alumni. Your alma mater might have established connections with companies and employers who already have work-from-home jobs but even if they do not have such a position yet, the company or employer may create one, so that they could hire more people from your alma mater based on the strong and positive track record of hiring people from your school.

Bring your resume and cover letter in-person: It sounds old-fashioned, especially in this day of technology and online job sites, but it is still one of the best things to do. Why? Because you will not be a faceless person on a mile-high stack of online resumes. Rather, the manager will be able to put a nice face to the name on your resume and cover letter and will see that you are very interested in the position and company as you made time in your busy schedule to come in-person. And that speaks volumes. And that manager might already ask you a few questions or if it goes really well, schedule an interview for the following week. Just a few words of caution: do not walk into the company office just before lunch or five minutes before everyone goes home, expecting for the manager to have time and be happy to see you. It just will not leave a good impression or work too well, either.

Library: Check with your library to ask and learn more about available job and remote work search resources. Librarians may also be able to suggest other helpful tools such as workshops, brochures, books, and websites.

Employment agency/Job resource centre: Contact employment agencies and job resource centres to find information on what they offer. They may know about remote work job postings, interviews, and career fairs or direct you to other places and contacts.

Join sports clubs and interest groups: If you like to play a sport, then join a tennis club, fencing club, soccer, basketball or baseball team. Get to know the other team players and club members and as you do so, let them know what kind of work you are looking for and what kind of work experience you bring to the table (this is a good time to have your elevator pitch ready). The people you talk to might know friends whose companies are hiring and can recommend who you should address your cover letter to or ask for an interview or maybe even just arrange a time to meet for coffee with the hiring manager.

Having a common interest with others can establish a basis for building a mutually beneficial friendship. It might not happen right away, when joining a sports club or team, that you will be able to see any potential job leads come your way but if you give it some time, you will most likely learn about new opportunities over time.

Book Club Discussion Guide

1. What fears and obstacles are faced in working from home? How can they be overcome?

2. What type of business structure may be the best – free-lancer, sole proprietor, corporation, partnership?

3. After reading the **Marketing and Finances** chapter, what are one or two actions to be taken in your finances? In marketing?

4. Describe your home office. What do you love about it? Is there anything that needs to be changed to create a more ideal work environment?

5. Are you confident in your technology skills? If not, what steps can you take to acquire the needed skills?

6. Are there steps you need to take to look after your health and have a healthy home environment from which to work in?

7. Which of the suggestions and ideas in the chapter **Working from Home for Life: Suggestions for Different Ages and Stages** did you find to be most practical and helpful? Were any of the suggestions and ideas new to you?

8. If you do not work from home but know others (friends, family, neighbours) who do, what are practical ways you can support and encourage them?

9. Which interview in **Part 2: Extraordinary People Who Work from Home** did you learn from the most or find most inspiring? What did you learn?

10. What goals might be made in working from home? How can working remotely help someone reach their goals?

A Little Help from Friends and Readers

I appreciate the support and help from friends, readers, and fans alike!

If you enjoyed this book, please leave a review on Amazon.com or Amazon.ca by going to this book's page or visit my author page. Even a short review, of one or two sentences, would be a great help. Reviews help others find out about and learn more about my book.

To follow along on my writing journey, I hope you will visit my website www.barborigarnet.com and join by subscribing to my e-newsletter.

Thank you!
Barbori Garnet

Index

Acknowledgements

Thank you to everyone who contributed to this book by sharing their work-from-home journeys, experiences, wisdom learned and gained over the years, and photos of inspiring work-from-home spaces. Your time, effort, and thought put into your responses is much appreciated. This book would not be the same without your contributions.

To the readers of this book, I hope you learn much from the information presented and shared and that you choose to take action to make working from home happen for you. Working from home means that you are taking a certain step toward freedom by freeing yourself from commuting by vehicle or public transportation to an employer's office every day. By taking this step, it might lead you to take other powerful and impactful actions.

My biggest thanks goes to my mom (who is also an author and illustrator), Barboria Bjarne, who knows just how much time, effort, concentration, perseverance, persistence, and passion goes into the making and publishing of a book. She guided me through every step of the way with her advice and wisdom. Thank you for everything!

And thank you to Atmosphere Press for helping to bring my book to life. It has been a wonderful experience working with the team at each stage along the path to publication.

About Atmosphere Press

Atmosphere Press is an independent, full-service publisher for excellent books in all genres and for all audiences. Learn more about what we do at atmospherepress.com.

We encourage you to check out some of Atmosphere's latest releases, which are available at Amazon.com and via order from your local bookstore:

Out and Back: Essays on a Family in Motion, by Elizabeth Templeman

Just Be Honest, by Cindy Yates

You Crazy Vegan: Coming Out as a Vegan Intuitive, by Jessica Ang

Detour: Lose Your Way, Find Your Path, by S. Mariah Rose

To B&B or Not to B&B: Deromanticizing the Dream, by Sue Marko

Sacred Fool, by Nathan Dean Talamentez

My Place in the Spiral, by Rebecca Beardsall

My Eight Dads, by Mark Kirby

Dinner's Ready! Recipes for Working Moms, by Rebecca Cailor

Vespers' Lament: Essays Culture Critique, Future Suffering, and Christian Salvation, by Brian Howard Luce

Without Her: Memoir of a Family, by Patsy Creedy

Emotional Liberation: Life Beyond Triggers and Trauma, by GuruMeher Khalsa

About the Author

Barbori Garnet is a writer, artist, musician, and gardener based in Alberta. She enjoys writing non-fiction and writes on remote work, home offices, gardening, and more. *Home at the Office: Working Remotely as a Way of Life* is her first book.

Barbori has worked from home since 2010, enjoying the flexibility and creativity it offers. Over the years, she has learned from others who work remotely and is inspired by their advice, stories, and suggestions.

Visit her online at www.barborigarnet.com.

CPSIA information can be obtained
at www.ICGtesting.com
Printed in the USA
LVHW070255030822
725079LV00022B/1281

9 781639 882687